DIALECTICAL METHOD OF MARX AND ENGELS

Geo Jomaria

Independently published

Copyright © 2022 George Joseph M

All rights reserved

No part of this book may be reproduced, or stored in a retrieval system, or transmitted in any form or by any means, electronic, mechanical, photocopying, recording, or otherwise, without express written permission of the publisher.

ISBN: 9798367746150
Imprint: Independently published

Cover design by: Art Painter
Library of Congress Control Number: 2018675309
Printed in the United States of America

To Late Dr. D. Alex

*I cherish your encouragement
from our first meeting to the last.*

CONTENTS

Title Page
Copyright
Dedication
Introduction   2
Chapter 1   8
Chapter 2   13
Chapter 3   20
Chapter 4   25
Chapter 5   31
Chapter 6   38
Chapter 7   46
Chapter 8   54
Chapter 9   65
Chapter 10   73
Chapter 11   79
About The Author   90

CONTENTS

Introduction

Chapter 1   Marxism: A Summary

Chapter 2   Dimensions of Dialectics

Chapter 3   Dialectics of Critical Negation and the Affirmation

Chapter 4   Dialectics between Awareness and Action

Chapter 5   Dialectics between Theory and Practice

Chapter 6   Dialectics of Accumulation of Capital

Chapter 7   Dialectics between Base and Superstructures

Chapter 8   Dialectical Logic of Successive Stages of History

Chapter 9   Iron Law of Capitalist Dialectics

Chapter 10 Dialectics between State and Civil Society

Chapter 11 Dialectics of Dictatorship of the Proletariat

INTRODUCTION

Dialectics is one of the most influential concepts in the European thought, especially after its usage by Hegel. Following the Young (Left) Hegelians, Marx and Engels discovered it in history, and popularized its contextual application. The objective of the book is to explicate how the concept of dialectics is implied and operated in different themes of Marx and Engels. Since Marx and Engels complemented each other in developing the philosophy and organizational strategies of scientific communism, the Marxian scholars treat them together as its authentic source and inspiration. All their works have got the same focus and conclusion. Even their independent works with different approach and style did not differ in concept. Many Marxist scholars divided the process of their philosophical growth into two periods, namely, early Marx and mature Marx. It was done on the basis of their gradual realization of the materialist conception of history. But the author of this book claims the presence of the concepts of mature Marx, especially the dialectical interaction of worker as the source of development, in their early works, and considers work as the link between both the periods.

The first two chapters, one on "A Summary of Marxism" and another on "The Concept of Dialectics", are introductory in nature. They help the readers to enter into the nuances of dialectics as applied by Marx and Engels. Rest of the chapters deal with dialectics in different contexts explaining important themes of Marxism. The first chapter treats 'work' as the central theme of Marxism and 'worker' as the subject of history and development. Engels, from the anthropological perspective, claimed that the tool handling is a unique capability of human hand that makes the humans workers. Humans, through laboring, developed their faculties, capabilities and surroundings. Labor facilitates humans to interact dialectically with their material living conditions and create a world of human need and taste. According to Marx and Engels, the workers who alter raw materials for the benefit of all have to intervene in the social living conditions and transform them for the welfare of all.

Hegel's concept of dialectics created great interest among the post Hegelian thinkers and altered the pattern of modern thought. Dialectics is the inner principle of motion and revelation. The process of development and method of understanding are dialectical. Contrary to the traditional and modern metaphysical position, Hegel reasoned the nature of being as becoming, truth as synthesis of contradictories and reality as coexistence of opposites. The second chapter deals with how the concept of dialectics was maturing in the thoughts of Marx and Engels. Initially, they were Hegelians with left orientation. As Young Hegelians, they were fascinated by the concept of dialectics and used it as a critical tool, especially against religious concepts. Later, as scientific communists, they applied it in the understanding of society in relation to its economic structure and proposed the scope of dialectics as a means for social transformation.

The third chapter treats dialectics as the critical negation of those concepts that are usually projected as real. The purpose of dialectical strategy is to affirm those realities that are conventionally negated. *Contribution to the Critique of Hegel's Philosophy of Law (Critique of Hegel's Philosophy of Right)*, written in 1843 by Marx at the Young Hegelian influence, was his most popular work on religious criticism. Marx and Engels borrowed Feuerbach's method of dialectical inversion that substituted the conventional subjects with their objects. For example, the creator God that was created by humans through self-alienation, was substituted with the creative power of humans. Later, in the process of discovering materialist understanding of history, Marx moved away from the Young Hegelians including that of Feuerbach by criticizing them as ideological, because their ahistorical explanation of human reality was hiding "the simple fact, ..., that mankind must first of all eat, drink, have shelter and clothing, before it can pursue" all other things. Hence, he began to explicate knowledge in the historical context and insisted upon the transformative task of philosophers.

The fourth chapter studies the initial attempts of young Marx of analyzing political economy. *The Economic and Philosophic Manuscripts of 1844,* one of his early works that became very popular among humanist Marxists much after his death, described human nature as self-reflective and dynamic labor. But the dynamic labor happened to be the source of alienation of workers under capitalism. Marx highlighted it as a process of impoverishing of workers while improvising the world. Every progressive step was regressive with regard to workers. Alienation causes the polarization between the class of thinkers and the class of workers. It vanishes only in a classless society where all members happen to be thinking workers.

The fifth chapter on the "Dialectics between Theory and Practice" begins with a treatment on the intellectual and organizational collaboration between Marx and Engels. The three famous works introduced in this chapter, *Theses on Feuerbach*, *The Holy Family or Critique of Critical Criticism* and *The German Ideology* (of which the last two were written jointly by Marx and Engels), deal with the development of the materialist conception of history. Marx and Engels attacked the ideologies of left Hegelians and English political economists who derived their theories of liberation or welfare society from the thought of other great thinkers and not from the social conditions of the most oppressed and the exploited. A theory of liberation unconnected with the material conditions of living cannot have clear action plan. According to Marx and Engels, the proletariat should be revolutionized with the philosophy of liberation, and the philosophy of liberation should find its material weapon in the proletariat. Thus, they discovered the dialectical philosophy of revolution through the synthesis of theory and practice.

The sixth chapter deals with different types of capital and different forms of accumulation. Different types and forms were determined by different means of oppression and exploitation. In all situations, the dialectical relation was between the appropriators of production and the real producers. The chapter also enquires on the origin of money as aggressive source of accumulation. The study is based on the *Capital,* the magnum opus of Marx.

The seventh chapter on "Dialectics between Base and Superstructures" treats Marxism as a philosophy of Economics. *Socialism: Utopian and Scientific of Engels, a* popular socialist pamphlet, provides the theoretical foundations of the philosophy of Economics. The whole society is imagined as a structure with the economic activities as its foundation and the state, morality, religion etc., as its superstructures. The economic factors of society are treated as the most significant elements of society that shape the structures and functions of all other social organizations. Hence, a revolutionary transformation of society is heavily depending on the radical transformation of its economy. Accordingly, Marx and Engels theorized a revolutionary dialectics beginning with the inner conflict in the economic foundation between forces of production and relations of production.

The eighth chapter enquires on the Marxian historiography. Marx and Engels explicated the trajectory of history as dialectical and progressive as seen in the successive stages of European history. They expounded the occurrence of successive leap in history due to the revolution in the mode of human interaction with the material conditions of living. Accordingly, historical periods, one after another, underwent epochal transformation with the revolutionary change first happening in the forces of production of each period. The insights of the chapter are derived from the *Preface to A Contribution to the Critique of Political Economy* by Marx and the *Origin of Family, Private Property and State* by Engels. The chapter analyses the Marxian claims on the existence of primitive communism and the prediction on the advent of scientific communism.

The chapter nine on the "Iron Laws of Capitalist Dialectics" deals with the rigid and flexible understandings of dialectical trajectory of successive stages of history. This is one of the most disputed Marxian concepts. Marx, in his "Preface to the first German Edition" of the first volume of the *Capital,* predicted that it was natural for the industrially advanced England to move to its next stage as dictated by the iron laws of nature. Many Marxists understood the revolutionary leap to communism as universal, uniform, single-linear and progressive, and hence, expected automatic emergence of communist society. The optimistic prediction of the strategist of revolution created docility instead of enthusiasm among revolutionaries. Therefore, Marx and Engels reoriented workers to be the creators of history and establish communism. Hence, they recommended context-based paths to communism.

The tenth chapter explains the dialectics between state and civil society. Hegel conceived state as the highest manifestation of Spirit appeared for solving conflicts in civil society and establishing social order. Marx critically observed the state as the alienation of civil society. The conflict in civil society continued and state functioned as the protector of the interests of the dominant group for creating favorable conditions for exploitation.

The last chapter deals with dialectical conflict within the revolutionary process, and the dichotomous existence of the dictatorship of the proletariat. Marx proposed dictatorship of the proletariat in the *Critique of the Gotha Programme* as a workable post-revolutionary administrative structure to protect and promote the revolutionary cause against the adventurism of statelessness of the anarchist philosophers. It follows constructive and persuasive dialectics.
Engels, in the Introduction to Marx's *The Civil War in France,* showed some of the strategies and guidelines implemented by the revolutionary Paris Commune as models of the dictatorship of workers.

This book is introductory and textual. The conceptual jargons are explained in simple language. All claims are made with reference to the original works of Marx and Engels. In each chapter, one or the other major classics of them are introduced along with the context of writing them. The works of the later Marxist thinkers and other secondary sources have influenced the author, but none of them are used to substantiate the claims. This book is the outcome of many years of teaching of philosophy in Arul Anandar College, Karumathur, Madurai, Tamil Nadu, India, and I express my gratitude to my students, colleagues and members of the college management. I specially thank late Prof. D. Alex, my mentor, and Rev. Dr. Elphinstone Kishore for correcting the manuscripts.

CHAPTER 1

MARXISM: A SUMMARY

Work is the central theme of Marxism and worker is the subject of history. The human ability for working was evolved gradually, and stimulated the organic development of all faculties. Frederick Engels substantiates it in his essay *The Part Played by Labour in the Transition from Ape to Man* based on the anthropological findings. "Labour is the source of all wealth, the political economists assert. And it really is the source- next to nature, which supplies it with the material that it converts into wealth. But it is even infinitely more than this. It is the prime basic condition for all human existence, and this to such an extent that, in a sense, we have to say that labour created man himself."[1] The physical structure of human beings that are suitable for tool handling was evolved through adaptation while encountering with the hard conditions of nature. Engels, in detail, narrated the development of human hand as the first radical step to the evolution of human being. "But the decisive steps had been taken, *the hand had become free* and could henceforth attain ever greater dexterity; the greater flexibility thus acquired was inherited and increased from generation to generation. Thus, the hand is not only the organ of labour, *it is also the product of labour.*"[2] The new operations of human labor initiated further development of all other organs, changing the patterns of muscles, ligaments, bones and so on. Thereafter, the organs of mouth gradually learned to pronounce distinguishable sounds. Creative activities of human body through work and sound sharpened brain, refined senses, advanced consciousness and improved relations leading to the appearance of "fully-fledged man" living in society. With the evolution of organs, humans began to interact with natural surroundings innovatively, and modified them to be suitable for their living. Human labor created a world that fulfilled human needs and tastes.

Marx discovered conscious labor as the starting point and the driving force of human development. But the creative work is a source of enslavement in an antagonistic society. The more the workers contribute the more they are alienated. Capitalism was the most deeply divided society and it was under capitalism, workers became most insignificant. Marx and Engels contemplated on remedial measures and workable strategies of correction. Marxism, thus, is a critical and contextual enquiry into the oppression and the exploitation of human labor under the existing mode of production and an actual effort to develop transformative strategies for the liberation of the oppressed and exploited workers. Indirectly and in the long run, Marxism aims to regain for all human beings their original nature of conscious labor along with improved living conditions.

The primary task of human labor is the production of necessary goods for immediate consumption for survival. An activity of plucking or taking and eating a fruit from forest involves choice-based labor. It is not simply an accidental act but purposive. The choice is determined by the context of the person who chooses. One can decide whether to pluck this fruit or that, but only from the available fruits. One can also be satisfied with a fallen fruit. Labor is not simply limited to the acts of survival. The scope of labor is extended from the means of subsistence to the laying of the foundation of human history and functioning as the creative force of all development. Marx and Engels affirmed that work was the foundation of all development, and human history had been built on the shoulders of workers. The human labor that was conscious in the natural order is blindfolded in the divided societies to be directed by the crooked dominance. In an antagonistic society, people who apply their labor power to make and move history are not regarded for their worth and contribution. On the contrary, those who enjoy the products of labor of somebody else are rewarded with the title of producers or creators of history.

During the initial periods of evolution of labor, the primitive technologists supplemented the laboring hand with crude tools and rough implements. Augmentation of human abilities and reduction of hardships of work were the purposes of technology. Technological advancements reinforced human hand and expedited human brain in converting or extracting natural resources. Hence, forces of production which include means of production, raw materials and labor force received much attention, positively to their augmentation and negatively to their exploitation. Human is the only being that seeks never ending and ever-growing ranges of gratification. Moral and political thinkers are proposing regulative principles to curtail self-interest so that the output of developing forces of production may be made available to all. The systems and regulative principles of linking the forces of production with society at large are called relations of production. Relations of production institute regulative systems of linking different components of forces of production like relation of workers with raw materials and tools. Under feudalism peasants were tied to land and manufacturers were bound by guild system. Similarly, relations of production establish the systems of linking goods and services with the needy like free market system under modern capitalist economy. Relations of production maintain relations among different categories of people and societal facilities by regulating and operating the productive and distributive systems and principles. The forces and relations of production together form the economic base of a society.

The consequences of unbridled extension of human endeavor for gratification affect relations among humans and also with their environment. Thus, the relations of production are considered as worrisome domains of human activities. Under capitalism free market system functions as the relations of production that regulate the provision of goods, services and facilities only on payment. Earning profit is the only regulative principle of free market relations of production. Overproduction steered by the blind market, selective provisions only to the moneyed consumers, appending of political, social, cultural and legal systems to the market forces, free flow of insecure and unemployed laborers for exploitation and expanding and destructive technologies are some of the features and consequences of market driven economic system.

In society, there are certain types of regulative systems other than the relations of production that are also influencing the living conditions. Marx and Engels identified those social institutions like state, religion, laws, moral norms, etc. as extra-economic social structures. Accordingly, they classified the social structures into two levels similar to a construction: economy as base structure and the rest as superstructures. Forces of production and relations of production are the two dialectical components of economic base. Superstructures like state, religion, morality and law are constructed on economic structure. In each stage of history, economic mode is the deciding factor of societal functions and relations. Superstructures are periodically tuned by economic base, and they, in turn, bend themselves to serve the economic interests of the exploiting class. Hence, superstructures are suspected to be instruments of dominant class.

Marx and Engels claimed dialectics as the dynamic nature of interconnected reality. Dialectics is also considered as the methodology of understanding the dynamic and interrelated reality. The reality moves, and the driving force of movement is conflict. It is the interaction within the reality. Work is the mode by which humans dialectically interact with nature and that is the source of all development. Humans critically or innovatively interact with the conditions of living and convert the unbearable living conditions conducive for comfortable living. Workers who convert miserable conditions of living to comfortable conditions are in misery. The materialistic conception of history reveals the reasons of their enslaved conditions and proposes strategies of liberation. A revolutionary theory is aimless and ineffective without committed bearers of it. Marx and Engels wrote volumes and participated in the organizational activities to ignite the spark of transformative dialectics of social revolution in the minds of those who are transforming raw materials into commodities and augmenting private property for the capitalists.

CHAPTER 2
DIMENSIONS OF DIALECTICS

The intensity of intimacy between lovers increases with the resolution they make after every quarrel. If the quarrel is perceived as a separate act independent of reconciliation, love making becomes a boring impossibility. Synthesis of opposites creates conducive conditions for budding and growing. Conflict is constructive.[3] Dialectics is the inner principle of motion and revelation. It is the process of growing and method of understanding, and explains the progress in reality and knowledge. Hegelian dialectics challenged the modern concept of static nature of reality and truth. Mind, the reality, reveals itself to the ordinary minds as dialectically and progressively evolving. The kinetic reality appears as 'it is' and 'it is not' at the same time. Therefore, one is at the same time 'one' and the 'other'. With Hegel, *becoming* became the nature of being, and *truth* became transitory. On the contrary, traditional logic trained our minds to perceive object of knowledge as static and one as different from the other and also independent of the other. As the traditionalists, the modernists also were conservatives in their belief on the static nature of reality and truth. Truth is one only, and between contradictories both cannot be true. The reality is there in the outside world as the object of knowledge independent of knowing persons with its permanent and unchanging natures and therefore the truth about the reality is one and permanent irrespective of the context of knowing. Hegelian dialectics challenged the scientific modernist and conventionalist truth claim.

Hegelian concept of dialectics made profound influence on Marx and Engels right from the days they associated with the Young (Left) Hegelians, and later, as historical materialists, they developed it into an effective methodology of social analysis and social transformation. Dialectics was an ancient philosophical concept used for explaining the dynamic nature of reality.

"This primitive, naïve but intrinsically correct conception of the world is that of ancient Greek philosophy, and was first clearly formulated by Heraclitus: everything is and is not, for everything is fluid, is constantly changing, constantly coming into being and passing away."[4] Engels praised Greek philosophers as 'born natural dialecticians'. Socrates, Plato and Aristotle extensively applied dialectics at different domains. Engels gave prominence to Aristotelian dialectics as he applied it to explain change in the biological organism. Among modern philosophers, Engels regarded Descartes and Spinoza as brilliant exponents of dialectics. But modern philosophers set aside dialectical reasoning due to the influence of the laws of physical sciences. Similarly, French materialists also preferred metaphysical mode of reasoning to dialectical reasoning, because they did not notice the evolutionary character of reality. They understood the movement of matter as mechanistic and its nature as static. Kantian antinomies dealt with opposites but only to limit the scope of knowledge within the domain of appearance. There was no scope for transcending or transforming the appearance. Towards the end of modern philosophy, Hegel revolutionized dialectics as the nature of dynamic, all-encompassing, all-pervading, all integrating and all comprehending One, the Being. Being lives in mutation. Organic being is not a static or dead being but living and growing being. Hegel substituted the static being of the traditional metaphysics with dynamic being of transcendence, always changing. Being is no more an unmoved mover, but a vibrant and active moving mover, discovering, revealing and innovating through horizons of new manifestations.

We may perceive many parts or differentiating natures and opposing qualities in a being. They are inseparable. Though they are opposed, they interpenetrate as one. Magnet exists only with positive and negative poles. They are interrelated and interconnected. No part is independent of any other part or independent of the whole being. Similarly, no part can be known independently of other parts. An organic being cannot be segmented, but we may be able to comprehend and name different structures and functions of being as parts. For e.g., human being has different parts like hand, leg, eyes etc. Are they different parts or only different names using to understand organically interconnected structures and functions of a human being? No part has got existence or activities independent of the whole being. Being is becoming and becoming is the expression of being. Formal logic cannot understand the coexistence of contradictions. Only dialectical reasoning can reveal the 'is and is not' of the reality at the same time. The dialectics of reality is comprehensible as existing with opposites. All interconnected opposites are not independent and therefore cannot be known through metaphysical reasoning that treats one as identical and different from other independent identities. Metaphysical understanding restricts the knowledge of being within the definable permanent essences and attributes. Being is eternally condemned to be static with no scope for innovation and progress.

Dialectics is the means by which being reveals and realises itself. By revealing, it realizes. Hence, being is a progressively ever-changing reality, revealing and realizing itself. "Dialectics ...comprehends things and their representations, ideas, in their essential connection, concatenation, motion, origin, and ending."[5] Being is in transcendence. It surpasses its oneness by revealing its opposing principles in the process of creating its path for the realization of its transcending existence. Being travels through its opposing characters and reveals dichotomous aspects and reconciles at a transformed point of existence and experience. The process is expressed with the triad of dialectical logic, namely, thesis, antithesis and synthesis. While 'I am', I am also 'I am not'. While I understand myself as self-existence, I also understand myself as existing in relation to other selves.

Dialectics within being makes it dynamic. Being, the fullness as the affirmed, is challenged by its opposite, the nothingness as the negated. It is a kind of self-criticism, negatively the realisation of its limit, and positively the discovery of its possibilities. The being makes decision and exerts effort to overcome its limitation and seeks its possibilities. We may be able to explain it with an illustration of mental process. If the equanimity of a person is challenged by guilt, the person is troubled by internal conflict. The split or conflict can be resolved only if the cause of guilt is properly addressed. It is a corrective measure or self-improving process that has inward analysis and outward modification. They are not separate or independent acts. When the being is challenged by its non-being, being reaches to non-being through dynamic self-transcendence and becomes a new being incorporating appropriate elements from both being and non-being of the prior stage. Though the old is present in it, it is totally new, because the evolved being exists with new features different from that of the previous stage. Capitalism emerged from feudalism and retained some of the feudal traditions in it. But they resonate capitalist features, and abide by capitalist principles.

Everything is active and self-accelerated. All are potential projections. They are driven from within in response to their contextual conditions. Dialectical process is the dynamic path of all and dialectical means is the epistemological process of knowing all. Claims and counterclaims are settled in a synthesis incorporating the best from the process that suits to the situation. Contradictions can coexist as harmonizing elements in the synthesis until a new conflictual extremity comes into forefront. Being enters into a new dialectical process towards an innovative occurrence. Hegel applied dialectics on the traditional metaphysical polarities as coexistence of opposites like matter and mind, good and bad, positive and negative, being and nothingness. When they are treated as independent entities or concepts, they are existing as irreconcilable dichotomies. Negation of reality is not an absolute exclusion of reality but the affirmation of the limit of reality to show its possibilities. Tree is not the emptying of seed, but the revelation of the potencies of the seed. Thus, negation is not the denial of reality but revelation of the opportunities of reality. Conceptually negation refers to the opposite with includable tendencies and existentially they coexist as opposites like positive and negative poles of a magnet. Self-activated, interactive and progressive becoming of claims, meanings, truths or realities may be demonstrated with an example of a discussion in a class. Participants of the discussion may provide interesting insights, critical remarks or provoking reactions. None of them go in vain, because they may further activate and enrich discussants and develop knowledge. The triad need not be considered simply as a three-step process towards synthesis but emerged from divergent possibilities. Plurality of fuel makes fire.[6]

Hegel applied the concept of dialectics on thought, experience, culture, institutions and history. His dialectical idealism influenced the German thought in various ways. According to Engels it penetrated extensively in the most diversified sciences and leavened even popular literature and the daily press, from which the average "educated consciousness" derives its mental pabulum."[7] The destiny of dialectics on German thought was dialectical dividing Hegelians into opposing camps with opposite interests like idealists and materialists, rightists and leftists and conservatives and liberals. Immediately after the death of Hegel, there were two Hegelian groups radically opposing each other: Right Hegelians and Left Hegelians. "And in the theoretical Germany of that time, two things above all were practical: religion and politics. Whoever placed the chief emphasis on the Hegelian *system* could be fairly conservative in both spheres; whoever regarded the dialectical *method* as the main thing could belong to the most extreme opposition, both in politics and religion."[8] The Right Hegelians derived conservative attitude from Hegel especially in admiring autocratic Prussian state as the apex of dialectical appearance of the absolute. The authoritative state was an embodiment of rational system that was beyond rational criticism and change. Hegelian idealism constructed a mammoth structure of the spirit in the world. The reason manifested as the supreme state by resolving conflicts in civil society. State was the highest manifestation of the spirit and human appearances were destined to fulfil the task assigned to them by the state. State as the highest synthesis in the world resolved all conflicts within by the resoluteness of spirit in the form of monarch. Dialectical dynamics of spirit was institutionalized in the static state. The conservative Hegelians opposed radical reaction against the state.

The left Hegelians who were popularly known as Young Hegelians, inspired by the revolutionary elements of Hegel, claimed that the dialectics was a continuous restless process creating space for criticism and revolutionary action. They questioned the dictatorial Prussian rulers and conservative and irrational religious authority. They challenged political and religious authorities and demanded them to be sensible to the ordinary minds. They recognized rational as real only so long as the real was rationally justifiable as suitable and necessary for the time. Once the reason was bound by the obsolete real, the reason had to break the fetters and show the path of liberation. State was not static but progressive appearance and revelation of reason. While the conservatives obstructed revelation of reason, (the) radicals complemented reason's self-revealing task. According to conservatives, absolute power was bestowed on state and ordinary minds had to adhere to authority. While the rightists religiously surrendered their freedom and obeyed authorities as the manifestations of spirit, the left wing, influenced by Hegel's concept of history as progressive realization of freedom, declared freedom against irrational dictates of authorities and God.

Marx and Engels, like other students of German universities, were fascinated by Hegelian philosophy via Leftist route. The prominent Young Hegelians were David Friedrich Strauss, Arnold Ruge, Bruno Bauer, Ludwig Feuerbach, Max Stirner, and Moses Hess. Karl Marx became member of the group while he was in the University of Berlin in 1836 at the age of 18, doing law and majoring in history and philosophy. Frederick Engels also was influenced by the teachings of Young Hegelians. They perceived the Hegelian theology of the world spirit as the culmination of religion in philosophy. Though the Young

Hegelian were mostly materialists and atheists, they derived their idea from idea only as Marx and Engels later criticized as idealist inclinations.

Marx and Engels, with the discovery of materialist understanding of history, criticized the Young Hegelians in 1844 in their collaborated work *The Holy Family, or Critique of Critical Criticism: Against Bruno Bauer and Company* and inaugurated the concept of historical materialism. While Hegelian dialectical being was idea or spirit, Marx and Engels relocated it in history. They began their enquiry not from abstractions of experience but from concrete experience. In *The German Ideology: Critique of Modern German Philosophy According to Its Representatives Feuerbach, B. Bauer and Stirner, and German Socialism According to Its Various Prophets* written around 1845, they disapproved the Young Hegelian shallow criticism and transformative action which were not properly contextualized to the actual situation of oppression and exploitation. Marx and Engels developed dialectical perception of material living conditions. They devised dialectics as a method of knowing, perceived it in history, saw it in nature and proposed it as transformative force.

CHAPTER 3
DIALECTICS OF CRITICAL NEGATION AND THE AFFIRMATION

Negation itself is an affirmation. A philosopher was born on May 5, 1818 at Trier in Germany to proclaim to the world "the simple fact, hitherto concealed by an overgrowth of ideology, that mankind must first of all eat, drink, have shelter and clothing, before it can pursue" all other things,[9] as told by Engels at the graveside of Karl Marx at Highgate Cemetery in London who died on March 14, 1883. Marx and Engels were in search of a new methodology for revealing the simple but hidden facts of human living. They started from the complex ideologies, critically approached them and incorporated them selectively for developing a methodology for the understanding and changing of the neglected conditions of the ordinary. They borrowed dialectics from Hegel and enriched it in association with the Left Hegelians who did not apply it at the right place. They found Hegel and the Left Hegelian thinkers were standing upside down. So, Marx and Engels decided to position them on their feet by bringing the dialectics down to the earth, and applied its dynamics in the understanding of the history of oppression and exploitation. They reoriented the methodological focus of dialectics in the way that it can be used for knowing, interpreting and transforming the cloudy realities that make human life hard and facilities inaccessible.

The Young Hegelians were interested in the conventional philosophical themes such as God and the relation of self and world with God. They criticized God, religion and authoritative institutions. Feuerbach's *Essence of Christianity* attacked the religious concepts from the materialist and anthropological perspectives, and that attack made tremendous impact on a large number of thinkers and activists. "One must himself have experienced the liberating effect of this book to get an idea of it. Enthusiasm was general; we all became at once Feuerbachians."[10]

Feuerbach regarded religion and theology as the products of self-alienation of human essence. He perceived the deification of human attributes as the source of God. The characteristics of divinity, such as providence, goodness, love, justice, holiness and so on were really the lost essences of humanity. What were expected to be with humans but wanting in human relationships were compensated with the belief in the relationship with God. Bonding with God was a blot to humanity.

Feuerbach tried to establish secular basis of theology by proposing human relations as the real subject matter of theology. The study of divinity should begin with its earthly realities. In this regard Feuerbach developed the method of inversion for reversing the projected ideas like that of God to their origins by disclosing their worldly roots. He argued that the Absolute Spirit of Hegel was "man's essence outside man". Feuerbach inverted conventional 'subjects' of metaphysics and theology by reversing them into 'predicates' and the metaphysical predicates into real subjects. He negated traditional subjects like God or spirit and affirmed human subjects as creative and revealing ventures. Inspired by Feuerbach, Marx pointed the Feuerbachian weapon directly at the 'gods of the world' and declared the presence of real creators of the world in the peripheries.

Contribution to the Critique of Hegel's Philosophy of Law[11] is a popular article written in 1843 by Marx at the Young Hegelian influence during his transition period to historical materialism and an *Introduction* to it was written in the following year. The *Introduction* is very famous for its description of religion as the opium of distressed people. In this article, Marx analyzed Hegel's political philosophy in the Feuerbachian manner. Marx criticized Hegel for being uncritically subservient to the Prussian state as the highest manifestation of spirit above civil society. Hegel considered the actual social relations and property relations existing in civil society as imaginary and on the contrary, the idea of state was taken as the real subject. "It is important that Hegel everywhere makes the idea the subject and turns the proper, the actual subject, …, into a predicate. It is always on the side of the predicate, however, that development takes place"[12]. According to Hegel state originated as the super mediator that overcame the conflict in civil society. But Marx derived its perverted origin in a divided society as an organ of coercion enforcing oppression and exploitation on behalf of the upper class.

Marx's critical re-reading of history was unique. According to him, the historians negated the real moving force of history with the pseudo forces. Marx blamed Hegel for placing the spirit as the force behind the evolution while it was occurring in the dynamic world thanks to human interaction. Hegel depicted the state and its monarch as the moving forces of world history while the history was built by the hard toil of workers. The Hegelian superimposition of spirit or god on the state was not the product of imagination but a purposive act demanding obedience to the political system and authority of his time. The worldly reality was expressed as transcendental reality, mostly as an alien spirit from which all laws and norms were accordingly evolved to be followed in the ordinary conditions of human relations. Thus, Marx wanted the Hegelian attempt of concealing the real carriers of human history by projecting the monarchs in their place to be reversed in theory and the real carriers to be brought forth from their oblivion through effective practice.

Marx and Engels were attracted to the Feuerbachian method of inversion of religious concepts and extended its scope to the analysis of material conditions of human life. Natural human attributes can be regained not merely by the understanding of estranged human attributes but by removing the material conditions of estrangement. "Thus, for instance, once the earthly family is discovered to be the secret of the holy family, the former must then itself be criticized in theory and transformed in practice."[13] Estranged human attributes can be regained, but not from God, because there is no God. The expropriated have to realize the expropriating conditions and the expropriated have to work for changing the expropriating conditions. Marx and Engels applied the dialectical method for reversing conceptual perversion and prepared its victims to overcome its impact. Hence, the negation is the affirmation of the negated. The dialectical process is complete in the removal of those conditions creating social division, oppression and exploitation.

Marx used the technique of reversal in his economic analysis as well. When the political economists recognized capitalists as the real producers, Marx reversed it and tried to prove that the workers were the real forces of production who were producing for the use of all. Workers were bought by capitalists and surplus labor was extracted from them to produce profit for the capitalists. Hence, Marx considered accumulated surplus labor as the source of private property. If workers were engaging themselves in the production only for the duration that was enough to produce sufficient to earn their livelihood as in the traditional society, no capitalist could earn profit. Capitalists exploited surplus labor time either by increasing the hours of the working-day or by reducing the socially necessary labor time by the use of improved techniques of production. Worker earned just the minimum wage absolutely required to keep the laborer in bare subsistence as a laborer. Workers were engaged to produce according to the scheme laid down by the capitalists to acquire as per their plan. By hard work, the proletariat could not earn any property for it, but earned for the capitalist. "Hitherto, the owner of the instruments of labour had himself appropriated the product, because, as a rule, it was his own product and the assistance of others was the exception. Now the owner of the instruments of labour always appropriated to himself the product, although it was no longer his product but exclusively the product of the labour of others".[14] The non-producing owner (capitalist) entered into repeated reinvestments of the appropriated and the accumulated surplus for the expansion of exploitation and the increase of profit. Marx wanted the negated to take the inversion of their negation as a tool for regaining their original status as real producers. Hence, they can work for total liberation.

Critical negation is a revolutionary strategy. It affirms the existence and importance of the negated that were obfuscated by ideological process. Ideologues conceal the real human conditions by the revelation of superfluous elements of human existence.[15] The German philosophers projected mind as the force behind the development of humanity, whereas, according to Marx, the real power that moved human history and thought was the productive material interaction by workers. Ideologists, by projecting the mind as the primary force, could subjugate the real producers as inferior to thinkers and planners.

CHAPTER 4
DIALECTICS BETWEEN AWARENESS AND ACTION

Karl Marx was a voracious reader and a continuous learner. He enrolled himself as a student of law at the University of Bonn, bonded with philosophy at the University of Berlin and continued PhD on *The Difference between the Democritean and Epicurean Philosophy of Nature* under the guidance of Bruno Bauer who was his personal friend from the Young Hegelian circle. His proposition that theology must yield to the superior wisdom of philosophy was not palatable to the conservative professors in Berlin, therefore he submitted it in a less conservative university at Jena and received his doctorate from the University of Jena in 1841. During the stay in Paris from 1843-1845 while working with Arnold Ruge as the co-editor of the journal *German-French Annals,* Marx befriended with radical workers who were exiled from Germany. He began to observe the course of industrial revolution and study newly emerging branch of knowledge named political economy seriously. His association with the exiled workers stirred his organizational impetus and his exposure to political economy streamlined his intellectual focus and rigor. They caused Marx's transition from his early Young Hegelian, humanist and radical liberal stage to the historical materialist perspective. Within two years, in collaboration with Engels, he articulated this conceptual change in *The German Ideology*. Marxist researchers named intellectual contribution of Marx and Engels up to the transition period as *early Marx* or young Marx, and after the discovery of historical materialism, their works were grouped under *mature Marx*.

Economic and Philosophic Manuscripts of 1844, a collection of notes prepared while studying political economy extensively, is considered as one of the most popular books written by Marx during the transition period. It was first published posthumously in 1932 from Moscow by the Institute of Marxism-Leninism.

Though the work is considered as belonging to the period of early Marx, the elements of historical materialism and different understandings of scientific communism were present in their seminal form in it. It became famous among the Western Marxists mainly for its treatment on human nature, estrangement of labor, individual tendencies and so on. These ideas influenced some of the twentieth century existentialists also.

Labor is the central theme of Marxism. Worker is the creator of human history and bearer of social development. We substantiated the above claims in the first chapter with suitable citations from *The Part Played by Labour in the Transition from Ape to Man*, an article published by Frederick Engels in 1878 from the historical materialist perspective. The young Marx formulated them in the *Economic and Philosophic Manuscripts of 1844*. He claimed that the labor was the dynamic nature of human being. "The whole character of a species – its species character – is contained in the character of its life activity; and free conscious activity is man's species – character".[16] As life originated from non-life, consciousness evolved from matter. Certain type of material interaction in an unknown time made a progressive negation in matter to the formation of consciousness as a revolutionary leap in the realm of reality. Human being as a conscious actor lives by free conscious interactions with the world around. Materialist conception of Marx affirmed labor as the self-fulfilling human capability and creative potency. The free conscious labor is a unique intrinsic quality of self-transforming human being. The purposeful, creative and productive labor progressively interacted with natural resources for satisfying human needs and that triggered the development of humanity. Whereas the animals repeat their past, humans, with their reflective labor create their future. "A spider conducts operations that resemble those of a weaver, and a bee puts to shame many an architect in the construction of her cells. But what distinguishes the worst architect from the best of bees is this, that the architect raises his structure in imagination before he erects it in reality. At the end of every labour-process, we get a result that already existed in the imagination of the labourer at its commencement".[17] Every human being as a reflective worker fulfils oneself only when one works as a free and conscious being. That is the way humans exceed themselves. The most astonishing miracle among natural wonders is the self-activated and self-involved human evolution while fatefully remaining as human being. When all other beings, if at all undergoing evolution, evolve into new beings, humans enter into self-created new conditions of living to participate consciously either to be the governors or the victims of evolved conditions. Self-actualizing human labor, under the conditions of bondage, used itself and the surroundings for destructive purposes.

Economic and Philosophic Manuscripts of 1844 portrayed the strange phenomenon of impoverishing of workers while improvising the world. Under capitalism, workers, with their hard toil served society, but with regard to them it operated in reverse order. Every progressive step in the social development was regressive to workers. Workers were losing their possessions and their selves while they were accumulating property and prestige for capitalists. Marx contextualized his study on the liberation of people to the material conditions of the oppressed and the exploited. "We proceed from an actual economic fact. The worker becomes all the poorer the more wealth he produces, … The worker becomes an ever cheaper commodity, the more commodities he creates. The devaluation of the world of men is in direct proportion to the increasing value of the world of things".[18] While workers were losing by doing work, the capitalists were gaining through the convenient reassignment of the tool handling role of human nature to the wage laborers. Later, in the *Capital*, Marx developed the concept of commodity fetishism based on his observation of the devaluation of producers against the increasing value of products.

In the *Manifesto* Marx and Engels identified the nature of oppression and exploitation of workers under capitalism as different from that of feudalism. However hard the working conditions of peasants in the feudal society, they enjoyed the pride of possessing their means of production. Capitalism liberated traditional manufacturers and peasants from their hardships and customary dictatorial conditions of living, but by making their means of production unsuitable to the capitalist conditions of production. Hence, they sold their means of production along with trashes and joined the industrial work force as wage laborers just for their subsistence. Marx accepted the claim of political economists that the sale was one sided, non-negotiable and irreversible. Workers were sold in the market like commodities whose value was determined by the market phenomena. There was no free sale but conditioned by demand and supply. Capitalists intervened in the market through foul means like induced migration and enforced slavery to reduce the price of workers to the bear minimum. Workers were compelled to sell whereas capitalists were free to choose. If the labor was not sold every moment, there was no chance of saving it and selling it later, as and when there would be demand for it. "Labour is life, and if life is not each day exchanged for food, it suffers and soon perishes".[19] Consequently workers accepted the concealed deal of conceding their right over their products to their buyers and to produce commodities in the name of buyers that were not to be used both by sellers and buyers of wage labor but to exchange in the market for profit. Hence, non-producers became real producers and sold the products under the brand designed by designers who had no copy right over the design and promoted by advertisers who could not ensure the quality that they were advertising. Under capitalist market conditions products were gaining name and fame in contrast to the thinning public presence of all who were associated with the making of products' public presence. Commodities in the department store appeared "as independent beings endowed with life, and entering into relation both with one another and the human race"[20]. Marx named the deification of human products in contrast to the devaluation of producers as fetishism of commodities. Money was the highest manifestation and supreme monarch in the hierarchy of fetishes recognized as the most respectful negotiator in the market that could climb the peak of success that no human person had ever scaled. The estranged workers surrendered their basic nature of thinking for doing and accepted animal nature of doing at the will of masters as normal and natural. Workers, who had owned labor power, means of production and the products of labor once, lost all to be kept alive in their revolutionary ambitions and nostalgic dreams.

The beginning of enslavement is associated with the dissociation of workers from the planning activity. Slave was better placed than the modern proletariat on account of slave's freedom of choice regarding the ways of work and tools of operation. Capitalism, the apex of antagonistic stages of development, stabilized extreme form of estrangement. The severity of alienation increases in the most developed societies because of the lopsided development. The underprivileged and under facilitated undergo severe perversion due to the deprivation of accessibility to the increased facilities. Workers who are on the peripherals undergo stress due to their inability of fulfilling increasing needs augmented by social development.

Marx observed that the humanity was polarized into two opposing classes under capitalism: decision making bourgeois class and determined proletarian class. Members of both the classes are deprived of being human as both are not able to fulfil their life as thinking workers. They compensate the unfulfilled domain elsewhere outside the sphere of their living conditions. Thus, social life itself becomes perverted and unsatisfactory. As they are unable to regain their human nature, they remain in the opposite camps as irreconcilable poles until they are forced to reconcile in a classless society having the material conditions for the realization of 'free conscious activity'. As the theory and practice are integrated in revolutionary praxis, consciousness and labor are synthesized in free conscious work. If the humanity is to be liberated from the alienated conditions of capitalism, a primordial synthesis between reflection and action in human person has to be reached in an advanced stage. In such a social stage all will be able to enjoy bourgeois facilities with the attitude of primitive communism. The polarization between the class of thinkers and the class of workers vanishes and merges into the humanity of thinking workers or conscious actors. We need a social situation where all can function as free conscious actors. Marx visualized classless society where all have the opportunity to work for the welfare of all.

CHAPTER 5
DIALECTICS BETWEEN THEORY AND PRACTICE

Marx and Engels critically reacted to the dominant philosophy of their time for not being sensitive to the miserable human conditions of their surroundings. Thought born out of thought takes thinkers away from human realities, but the thought resulting from the reaction to human conditions addresses human problems. Marx and Engels developed materialist conception of history as epistemological tool as well as strategic plan of action. They turned their attention against the ideas that were in vogue and learned from the living conditions of working class during the initial stages of industrial revolution. In the process, they studied political economy. They criticized political economists for accepting capitalist conditions as natural, and sought possible alternatives to capitalist economic system. The leap in the understanding of the materialist conception of history as a methodology of understanding, criticism and transformation occurred during their second meeting in 1844 in Paris. Two-year younger Engels, while returning from Manchester in England where his family had a textile unit, visited twenty-six-year-old exiled Marx. The first meeting of Engels with Marx in 1842 at the office of the *Rheinische Zeitung*, the liberal radical newspaper under Marx's editorship, was casual and unpromising. But the second meeting was rewarding. Both understood in the other the similar vision, focus, and intellectual commitment. They began their intellectual association and organizational collaboration with their joint venture of writing *The Holy Family, or Critique of Critical Criticism.* It was the first open declaration of their stand on the Young Hegelian critical tradition. Engels remained in Paris for ten days and finished his side of the contribution before leaving to his hometown Barmen in the Rhine Province of Germany. The book revealed their initial inclinations towards materialism, communism and political economy. Both of them together strengthened the sprout. They studied political economy, undertook expedition to industrial society for direct experience and interacted with the miserable conditions of workers. During the initial periods of their learning political economy, they separately undertook their intellectual endeavors. *Economic and Philosophical Manuscripts of 1844* that Marx had written mainly for self-clarification were later published by Marxist researchers in 1932 and became classic in one or the other respects. Engels' works *Outline of a Critique of Political Economy* and *The Condition of the Working Class in England* were tasty nourishments for their joint venture.

    Marx and Engels had collaborated again in the writing of *The German Ideology* as a two-volume edition during 1845-46 to propose the materialist conception of history as an alternative to idealist views of the Young Hegelian thinkers, mechanistic materialists and shallow socialists. But the manuscript was left unpublished to be 'attacked by the gnawing criticism of mice' due to antagonistic political atmosphere. A few pages of the original manuscript could not be traced. The fourth chapter of Volume II was published during their lifetime. Many chapters, at broken sequences, were published at different periods in different journals or books, and finally all were collected and published in 1932 from Moscow. Marx and Engels admired the Young Hegelians for their methodology of dialectical negation that they had applied against conservative Hegelians, absolutistic Prussian authority and irrational religion. But they criticized the Young Hegelians for idealizing and universalizing their philosophy of liberation without linking it with the living conditions of the enslaved. Their sympathetic approach to the oppressed and their anger against religious and political authorities were supported with wishful strategies. The thinkers of liberation failed to link their ideas of liberation with the people who had to be liberated. Their theory of liberation of the oppressed and the exploited did not address the real problems of the oppressed and the exploited. Marx and Engels contextualized their idea. Under capitalist mode of production, capitalist workers were the most affected, and therefore, a philosophy of liberation of the industrial working class was focused.

Marx and Engels brought out the mature phase of materialist conception of history by strengthening the philosophical perspective and practical method of liberation of the exploited through their meaningful interactions on economic, political and organizational affairs. At the consent of the members of the *League of the Just*, Marx and Engels converted it into *Communist League* by baptizing it with the unholy water of the materialist conception of history and drafted its policies and programs in *The Manifesto of the Communist Party* in 1848, focusing on the liberation of the working class and through it the liberation of all. In the Manifesto they applied the dialectical revolutionary theory with dynamic transformative action in the historical context of the origin and development of bourgeois mode of production. They successfully handed over their discovery to their dedicated followers who have been witnessing it in all corners of the world till today.

Marx and Engels applied materialist conception of history on all aspects of social relations, which started first with the critical introspection of their adherence to the Young Hegelian philosophy. They realized that the Young Hegelian theory of emancipation was not connected with living context and conditions of the oppressed and the exploited. The Young Hegelians were involving in superfluous philosophical criticism against exploitation and oppression, and Marx and Engels ridiculed their attempt as "child-like fancies". In the Preface to *The German Ideology,* the authors snubbed the Young Hegelians for making tall claims of imparting awareness on the oppressive ideas and authoritative dogmas with the expectation of radicalizing the enslaved towards their liberation. "Let us liberate them from the chimeras, the ideas, dogmas, imaginary beings under the yoke of which they are pining away. Let us revolt against this rule of concepts. Let us teach men, says one, how to exchange these imaginations for thoughts which correspond to the essence of man; says another, how to take up a critical attitude to them; says the third, how to get them out of their heads; and existing reality will collapse". [21] The Young Hegelians created a different system of ideas as critical force and tried to substitute the then existing set of ideas with their thought. But the basic structure and their conceptual framework were that of the old systems only. Marx and Engels attacked the Young Hegelians and other German critics for accepting the unexamined assumptions that had been taken from the idealist framework of opponents' thoughts. Hegelian philosophy was a kind of mystification unconnected with the worldly reality, but it imposed a world of its image on the worldly reality. The Young Hegelians were trapped in the Hegelian stalemate of situating human reality upside down. Once a system of thought was constructed, it continued to exist independent of the context of its origin. Thus the Young Hegelian philosophy was branded by Marx and Engels as German Ideology, because those thinkers failed to link their philosophy with German reality. Marx and Engels used the term ideology with a negative connotation indicating the construction of philosophical systems of human conditions on the foundations of thought and not derived from the real life-conditions of human living. "Every ideology, however, once it has arisen, develops in connection with the given concept-material, and develops this material further; otherwise, it would not be an ideology, that is, occupation with thoughts as with independent entities, developing independently and subject only to their own laws."[22] Hence, the Young Hegelians failed to contextualize the origin and existence of oppressive system in the material conditions of the oppressed. The ideas born out of ideas, instead of liberating the oppressed and the exploited, obstructed the process of emancipation. Their perceptions of the human problems diverted the attention of the affected from the real causes to less important or insignificant reasons. Historical materialist perspective of any issue is an attempt to understand them as they occur in the world, not in their abstract categories but as concrete realities. If the theory of liberation is conceived from moral, religious or political perspectives, independent of the material living conditions of the oppressed, it cannot see the core of the problems and solve. It is a partial view that cannot address the problems holistically, and consequently the target misfires.

That is why all who serve poor become rich, and there is no end for the misery of the miserable. Societal norms and laws are the convenient versions of the dominant "made - for - all" by keeping them under the veil of secrecy untouched by the ordinary. Though the dominant classes manipulate ideas to their favor, they make every effort to project them as good for all. "Your very ideas are but the outgrowth of the conditions of your bourgeois production and bourgeois property, just as your jurisprudence is but the will of your class made into a law for all, a will, whose essential character and direction are determined by the economical conditions of existence of your class."[23] A narrow point of view may be universalized by expressing it in the ideal form. Thus, a body of thought constructed by the universalization of partial or narrow perceptions is ideology. Under modern democracy, the programs that are most suitable for the advantaged are usually shown as the best for the most disadvantaged. For example, all the developmental activities that have been promoted by governments are said to be for employment generation. They are successful in establishing the superfluous link existing at peripherals as the most essential and needed. In short, ideology is false, because it is derived from wrong premises, manipulated, because it is fabricated from unexamined assumptions and purposes, because it is used as instruments of oppression and exploitation, yet it appears as though it is right, certain and workable.

In contrast to the German ideologists "which descends from heaven to earth", Marx and Engels advocated that knowledge should "ascend from earth to heaven."[24] It is a two-way process. Conceptions emerge from material conditions and grow to the level of transforming material conditions. In the traditional philosophical language, the dialectics of conception are intellect and will. Hence, conception implies understanding and doing. Source of our understanding is our interaction with our surroundings that in turn equip us with developed form of interaction with surroundings. Theory and practice are the dialectics operating within the philosophy of liberation. They coexist as the opposite poles relating to each other. Theory derives from the worldly realities, and enforces the worldly realities. A revolutionary theory is for a revolutionary action.

A revolutionary theory is intentional. It is the driving and guiding force of revolutionaries towards social transformation. Mere theoretical criticism of false ideologies cannot bring expected changes unless it initiates corresponding suitable and effective practices. The revolutionaries have to be engrossed with revolutionary theory. Regarding the relation between theory and practice, Karl Marx's aphoristic expressions in *Theses on Feuerbach* which he had scribbled down in 1845 for further elaboration came to be classical and famous.[25] He wrote eleven theses to attack the non-worldly character and idealistic inclinations of liberation theories that did not have appropriate action plan for the liberation of the oppressed and exploited. He affirmed the task of genuine thinkers in the eleventh thesis as follows. "The philosophers have only *interpreted* the world in various ways; the point is to *change* it."[26] Therefore, critical theory is not simply the critical awareness of false beliefs, but it is the transformative power of the oppressed and the exploited, and also of their volunteer-representatives. Accordingly, revolutionary theory is not an emotional outburst but properly planned means of deliberate action. "In the struggle against those conditions criticism is no passion of the head, it is the head of passion."[27] Its intention is not to make the metaphysical concepts clear, but to eliminate the oppressive system. For Marx, theoretical interactions were not for clarity of ideas and not even for objective knowledge but for preparing the proletariat for class struggle. Revolutionary theory is inevitable for radical action. Articulating revolutionary theory of the oppressed in the context of the oppressed preferably by the oppressed is ideal. But the theoreticians themselves are to be passionate with revolutionary theory and revolutionary action. Similarly, revolutionary action should be addressed to the oppressed, and it should be responded by the oppressed. Otherwise, the oppressed may continue to be submissive to the theoreticians and may be subjugated by the revolutionary leadership. Hence, synthesis between contextualized revolutionary theory and revolutionary action is necessary for social revolution. Some of the later Marxist thinkers named the synthesis between theory and practice as praxis: theory engaging in action. Practice unguided by theory is blind, and theory detached from practice is empty. Verbalism is mere theory which stands apart from human conditions of living, and activism is action without proper reflection and guidance. "The weapon of criticism cannot, of course, replace criticism by weapons, material force must be overthrown by material force; but theory also becomes a material force as soon as it has gripped the masses."[28] Marx was promoting neither verbalism nor activism but only self-conscious revolutionary action. A revolutionary should not be led by impulses. Marx considered philosophy as the head of the emancipation process while the proletariat was the heart of it. The proletariat is revolutionized by philosophy, and philosophy finds its material weapons in the proletariat. Theory is for practicing and the practice is to be based on theory. Theory and practice coexist in the dialectical philosophy of revolution.

CHAPTER 6
DIALECTICS OF
ACCUMULATION OF CAPITAL

The first volume of *Capital*, the magnum opus of Karl Marx in three volumes, was published in 1867 and the other two were edited by Engels and made available after the death of Karl Marx. The word 'capitalism' was an unfamiliar term for political economists including Marx. He usually used the phrases like 'capitalist mode of production' and 'bourgeois economy'. Later, the term capitalism was widely used both in Marxist and non-Marxist circles, attributing it to liberal bourgeois industrial economy. Private initiatives of the individual or corporate investors for the accumulation of profit through massive production and exchange through expanding markets. Adam Smith, the father of Political Economy and Scottish moral philosopher, enquired on the possibility of moral sentiments as the natural foundations of individual freedom, productivity, human happiness and harmonious society. Certain human traits such as greed, desire, etc. that were considered as vices by conventional morality became the moral drives of the altruistic action. The personal drive of acquiring for oneself became a beneficial source of public service. He brought out the links existing through individual freedom, personal efficiency, self-interest and useful economic activities. He affirmed natural and moral grounds of the capitalist economy. Marx observed it differently. Humans, left to themselves, are greedy, and therefore, their unregulated activities are inclined to be harmful to social order and common good. Marx was cautious of such human drives as greediness and self-interest, and therefore, he was critical of an economic system based on them. According to Marx, greed and self-interests are the driving forces of the unending urge for profit and accumulation and not service to others. Such an economy strives on by indulging in manipulation, oppression and exploitation.

    Capital was an innovative work dealing with different forms and stages of accumulation of capital and their impact on all forms of social relations and material conditions of living. The accumulation of wealth through plunder or other forceful methods and the use of them as the source of investment was named by Marx as the primitive accumulation of capital. Primitive accumulation was the original crude form of making wealth. The concept was discussed by Marx and Engels while dealing with the themes like estrangement, wage labor and proletariat. Original accumulation begins with the elimination of a group of people from their traditional means of production. In the beginning, a group of people or families held communal or common property as their private possession, and converted others landless and also slaves. Through war some were enslaved and used as unpaid workers. Similarly, during the emergence of capitalism, the means of production of guild manufactures and feudal workers were made useless by making their tools unproductive compared to the mechanized bourgeois instruments of production. As the guild manufacturers did not have enough wealth to invest in the advanced technologies of production, they were open to be bought as industrial wage laborers. On the contrary, the bourgeois, the class of non-producers, owned the means of production, producers and product. They produced qualitatively better products and encountered the traditional workers and manufacturers in the market with cheaper commodities, and more and more were added to the reserved army of the industries. The unemployed and estranged workers and manufacturers sold their labor power merely for their livelihood. Marx and Engels identified the specific nature of industrial workers as wage laborers who could survive only if they sold them in the job market and bought by capitalists.

    The initial capital was accumulated by the premodern exploiters, merchants and usurers. They who were part of the middle class in the Central and Western Europe entered into money earning circulations and accumulated money capital during the late medieval period. Money was just 'a money' only, a mere money. People sold their goods and received money and then purchased something else that was useful for them. Merchants and usurers converted into capital, an investment producing profit. They came to the market with money to buy commodities in order to sell them in the same market or elsewhere with a surplus rate. Usurers also accumulated wealth by lending money on inflated interest. The surplus money that they earned was added up to their investment of the previous circulations. "Money ends the movement only to begin it again."[29] The result of every circulation of commodities is the accumulation of money that returns to market as capital. With the development of technology, they found new opportunities of profit making in the mechanization of production process. They ventured into risk all their wealth in an area of unfamiliarity. They established new centers of manufacture and commerce outside the feudal boundaries and flourished as new entrepreneurs of the Mediterranean navigators and boat makers. Later they broke the feudal and guild fetters and liberated peasants and workers from the land and manufacturing units to which they were tied. They became the work force of the new commercial and industrial centers of strange and unreliable cities.

At the early stage of capitalism, the bourgeoisie rapidly accumulated capital by the use of dirty strategies of primitive accumulation. They plundered gold and silver of the West Indies at the extermination of natives, looted the wealth of the East Indies, commercialized agriculture, and enforced mining and industries on the shoulders of African slaves. All the above nourished capitalism in its childhood as the baby food and booster dozes. Such aggressive oppression and economic exploitation were the crude forms of primitive accumulation of capital that laid the foundation and drove the spirit of the most revolutionary and dynamic economy and society in the history of humankind. With the huge investment and the establishment of factories and through the extension of commerce, the bourgeois economy converted free laborers of the feudal society to wage laborers, goods to commodities and use value to exchange value. All productive and distributive relations were maintained and promoted only for increasing profit, amassing surplus value and for producing private property. Marx narrates the hardship of workers during primitive accumulation, "If money,…, "comes into the world with a congenital blood-stain on one cheek" capital comes dripping from head to foot, from every pore, with blood and dirt."[30] The cruel and refined faces of primitive accumulation continued in colonies and the colonisers annexed the colonies to perpetuate their exploitation and established imperialism at the global stage. While the imperialists represented enlightenment in Europe, followed all dirty strategies of primitive accumulation in the enslaved lands nakedly and shamelessly. They inflicted untold miseries on their native laborers to plunder their wealth. The natives objected in the beginning but accepted as there were no alternatives. Multinational companies and national commercial expeditions extended their empires to the corners of the world with the single purpose of plundering the wealth of generations and grew fat on the unpaid sweat and blood of colored skins, and a decent share of their swindle properly reached the chest of their countries and churches. European states approved racial and ethnic cruelties and fraudulent practices as legitimate and periodically encouraged. [31] The nexus between political dominance and economic establishments continues to legitimatize exploitation. Governments make policies to share public wealth with their favored capitalists in the form incentives, infrastructure and tax holidays and so on to boost individual efficiency. The most efficient among them come with nothing, show their entrepreneurship on the borrowed money, grow quickly or disappear fast, and appear in other nations to picture their nation with murky colors.

    Capital is money on expansion. It enters and withdraws with sole purpose of augmenting. The starting point of capitalist economy was commodity production or production for sale. In a non-capitalist society production was for immediate personal and local consumption that fulfilled human needs. Mercantile capitalism converted goods into commodities by superimposing exchange values on their use values. Money entered into market and gained the reputation of a feasible common scale to measure every commodity in the market and the worth of individuals in the economic and social ladder.[32]

Commodity production became capitalistic with the introduction technologically advanced machines in the manufacturing sectors that established large scale industries. Industrialization created new money-making opportunities for the bourgeois. The guild manufacturers with service mentality did not have the habit of saving money for further investment. Hence, they could not invest in large-scale industries. The bourgeois diverted money earning capital from mercantile activities to large scale industrial production. They pumped qualitatively better and cheaper commodities into market than the traditional manufacturers could do, and closed down their operations and joined as industrial workers in the modern factories.

Capitalism is an economic system that can function only on gain. In order to earn, the capitalist has to continuously and aggressively intervene in the expansion of their capital share and also their profit share. The investors' attitude underwent tremendous change. No longer they are satisfied with assured and predictable profit, but take pleasure in gambling in the economy of unseen treasures. The capitalists are excited with stress of risk and enthusiastic and optimistic during crisis as they are living in the glories of the future. Loss was tolerable though unbearable. Capitalism is the most aggressive economic systems in which all players have to enter into competition, conscious vigilance and merciless interactions.

Marx observed the credit system as a different source of accumulation of capital. The public debt becomes one of the most powerful levers of capitalist accumulation. Like a magnificent magician, the entrepreneur converts the barren money lying idle with the lazy massive and productive. Thus, "Public credit becomes the *credo* of capital."[33] With the introduction of banking system the industrial and commercial establishments are be treated as collective and public, functioning privately. Capitalism, thus, negated the collective nature of money gathered from people and converted into private property with the consensus of all. The stock-exchanges facilitate easy accumulation of capital for the capitalists and pleasure of gambling for the general public. Even in the loss, both the groups console themselves to wait for their next fortune.

Marx discovered the dialectical connection between accumulation and estrangement. The accumulation by capitalist was at the negation of means of production, indirectly livelihood, of the traditional manufacturers. They had no means for survival except that of selling themselves as wage laborers to capitalists. Capitalism as an economic epoch thrived with the active involvement of two dialectically opposing classes, on the one side, the bourgeois with the concentration of capital, means of production and dominance over decisions and on the other side, the proletariat with no means of subsistence, competing each other to actualize the desires and decisions of capitalists. Dialectics of primitive accumulation continues through naked oppression and exploitation in less developed countries and capitalist accumulation flourishes through subtle and veiled strategies of exploitation in advanced countries. And in developing countries both the forms are in operation simultaneously.

The political economists including Marx claimed that the surplus value was created by wage laborers. If they were producing commodities that were enough for their survival, capitalists could earn nothing. They produced much above the required production to earn their wage. The surplus production earned profit for the capitalist. Under capitalist mode of production, new values to the raw materials were added by workers. One who adds values can only create surplus value. It is unlike interest bearing capital that grows in time as trees grow in forest. Hence, Marx derived that the workers were the source of accumulation and expansion of capital.[34] In the traditional society work was the only source for the workers to earn the necessities for their survival. The surplus, if they were able to produce, had been appropriated by the ruling class. Under feudalism the serfs worked three to four days on their land and two to three days on the land of the feudal lord. The days that the serfs spent on their land were sufficient for them to produce their means of subsistence. Their surplus labor was the wealth for the feudal head. Similarly, capitalists extracted surplus labor time from workers above the necessary labor time either by increasing the hours of the working day or by reducing the socially necessary labor time by the use of improved techniques of production.

Surplus value is the source of accumulation and expansion of capital, and competition is their driving force. The aggressive tendency of expansion is an unavoidable feature of capitalism, and no capitalist choses it by his or her will, but to be compelled by the material conditions and social relations of production. Free choice on the basis of individual efficiency and inclination is determined by the inherent laws of capitalist production.[35] It is not because of the personal greediness that the capitalist accumulate wealth, but due to necessary greediness. "Use-values must therefore never be looked upon as the real aim of the capitalist; neither must the profit on any single transaction. The restless never - ending process of profit-making alone is what he aims at. The boundless greed after riches, this passionate chase after exchange-value, is common to the capitalist and the miser; but while the miser is merely a capitalist gone mad, the capitalist is a rational miser. The never-ending augmentation of exchange-value, which the miser strives after, by seeking to save his money from circulation, is attained by the more acute capitalist, by constantly throwing it afresh into circulation."[36] Whatever the bourgeoisie gains, is invested again in the same risky game. No capitalist can voluntarily give up ruthless exploitation and competition. Capital is always dynamic and creates surplus value in its each circulation. Capitalist enters and ever enters to create repeated surplus values; never returns, and if returns, it is only after total collapse. That is the clarion call inviting to the new era of history.

CHAPTER 7
DIALECTICS BETWEEN BASE AND SUPERSTRUCTURES

Engels was a continuous defender of scientific communism and historical materialism. For the general readers as well as for ardent followers, *Manifesto of the Communist Party* was sufficient to learn simple and clear idea about scientific communism. But many, including organizational intellectuals, deviated from materialist conceptions by interpreting communism from the idealist or mechanical materialist views. They imitated empirical science and conventional ways of thinking. Engels was compelled to give corrective additions to the philosophy as Marx was busy writing serious economic works. *Anti-Duhring* was written as a campaign against Duhring's shallow intellectual influence on the German Social Democrats. It was initially serialized in the *Vorwaarts,* the newspaper of the Social-Democratic Workers' Party, from 1877-1878, and then published as a book with the title *Mr. E. Duhring's Revolution in Science* in 1878 and later gained popularity as *Anti-Duhring*. In 1880, at Paul Lafargue's request, Engels rewrote three chapters of *Anti-Dühring* in the form of a propaganda pamphlet with the name *Socialism: Utopian and Scientific* for explaining scientific communism as an integral world outlook. It was a critical challenge to simplistic approach of socialist thinkers. *Socialism: Utopian and Scientific* became one of the most popular socialist pamphlets in the world at that time.[37] As the title refers, the pamphlet shows the fundamental difference between scientific socialism and utopian socialism. It brings out the historical role of scientific socialism. It unambiguously proclaims the materialist conception of history as the core of scientific communism. Engels considered it as one of the greatest discoveries of Karl Marx.

A comprehensive summary of materialist conception of history is given in *Socialism: Utopian and Scientific.* "The materialist conception of history starts from the proposition that the production of the means to support human life, and, next to production, the exchange of things produced, is the basis of all social structure; that in every society that has appeared in history, the manner in which wealth is distributed and society divided into classes or orders is dependent upon what is produced, how it is produced, and how the products are exchanged. From this point of view, the final causes of all social changes and political revolutions are to be sought, not in men's brains, not in men's better insight into eternal truth and justice, but in changes in the modes of production and exchange. They are to be sought not in the philosophy, but in the economics of each particular epoch."[38] Hence, Marxism is a philosophy of economics as a branch of knowledge dealing with the moving force of human history and society. It is the study on the general theory or laws of economic activities and their impact on individual and society with reference to the context of living. The primary economic activity consisted in human interaction with given material conditions to alter them for the use of humanity. Labor is the core of human relations among themselves and also with nature. Thus, the economic activity is treated as the base of society. All other achievements and developments of humanity are mainly dependent on economic aspirations and activities of humans. The production process is revolutionized with the increase in consumption, knowledge and skill.

According to materialistic understanding of history, a leap in history is the outcome of leap in the mode of production. Hence, successive stages of history are understood as caused by the revolutionary growth in the mode of production. Forces of production and relations of production are the dialectical segments of mode of production. Marx and Engels perceived society as organic and holistic which consisted of dialectical components of base and superstructures. They sketched the epochal transformation of society as triggered by the conflict within mode production that is between forces of production and relations of production. It culminates in the formation of new mode of production that consequently revolutionizes the relation between its base and superstructures. Base refers to the economic activities of production and distribution of goods. Human functions and relations are not limited to economic activities alone, but related to human culture and social regulations as well. For example, political relations, religious relations, legal relations etc. These secondary human relations are called superstructures. The analogy of base and superstructures is one of the most important concepts in the materialist analysis and understanding of social relations and social change.

Human history is filled with the narrations of vibrant activities and unforgettable events. They resurface in human life as glorious reminiscences and revengeful pangs. But none of them play any significant role in the epochal transformation unless it takes place in the mode of human interaction with material conditions of living. All other events and incidents are historical and memorable, and instrumental in making superfluous changes at peripheral levels. For example, invasions, ideologies, revolutions, disasters and great thinkers influence social change but substantial social transformation occurs only at the incidents of revolutionary change in the economic conditions.

The dialectical dichotomy dividing individuals at micro level reflects in the division of society into classes at macro level. Conscious activity or reflective labor is the nature of human being. In antagonistic society humans are divided into the class of reflecting humans and the class of laboring humans. Similarly, social functions and social institutions of a divided society are categorized into that which belong to superstructures and that which belong to economic foundation. Superstructures are ideological institutions erected on economic foundation but acting as the consciousness of society and functioning as if they are independent of the economic foundation. The laborers who shoulder the society remain invisible but the cosmetic ideologues, the superstructures, project their visibility as the bearers of social responsibilities. People usually enjoy a structure and judge it as good by seeing its elevation and color wash. Marx challenged the legitimacy claim of superstructures as independent while they were superimposed on economic foundation. "My investigation led to the result that legal relations as well as forms of state are to be grasped neither from themselves nor from the so-called general development of the human mind, but rather have their roots in the material conditions of life..."[39] Parallels may be drawn from the interdependence of base structure and superstructure to other concepts of dialectical coexistence between theory and practice, consciousness and action, vanguard and volunteers and so on. In an antagonistic society they behave as if mutually exclusive and in a non-antagonistic society they exist as interdependent. Accordingly, Marx and Engels targeted the Young Hegelians for not linking their revolutionary thoughts with the miserable living conditions of the oppressed and the exploited, and they turned to the study of political economy to identify the real causes of oppression and exploitation. Ideologists derived ideas from the thoughts of successive generations and failed to identify their origin in the material conditions of living. Thought begets thought and appears as the brain, nerves and backbone of society, projecting all economic activities as its products, hiding the contributions of real contributors.

Marx and Engels used the analogy of base-superstructure to express different types of relations of interdependence between economic conditions and regulative institutions of social relations. Common sensical understanding shows the fact that the strength, size and shape of a foundation determine the size and shape of superstructures. Marx, in his *Preface to a Contribution to the Critique of Political Economy*, treated the existence and forms of superstructures such as state, religion, family, social consciousness and so on which were conditioned or determined by the economic base. Marx and Engels discovered the law of revolution defining any revolutionary change in the economic domain as radically revolutionizing society in total. Accordingly, economic foundation as the cause and the moving power of history transforms not only economic base but also all superstructures. "Upon the different forms of property, upon the social conditions of existence, rises an entire superstructure of distinct and peculiarly formed sentiments, illusions, modes of thought and views of life. The entire class creates and forms them out of its material foundations and out of the corresponding social relations."[40] We may have to understand the Marxian analogy in the way that the superstructures or regulative institutions of society are constructed as social relations over economic activities and material facilities to influence them to be favorable to the advantaged. They behave as if they organize economic activities, material facilities and social relations for all but they really enter into justificatory communications in favor of the constructers. Therefore, radical solution to the social issues is to be sought and addressed comprehensively starting from the social organization of its economic affairs.

Base and superstructures of every epoch are dialectically synthesized. They remain in equilibrium with the tendency towards critical polarization waiting for the right conditions to express the contradictions of the equilibrated stage of history. Sprouting of seeds in the ripe time is a process of decay and growth. All structures are subdivided into their substructures existing either as synthesis or as opposites. The dialectical nature of the economic mode of production is illustrated through dialectical components of forces of production and relations of production. The forces of production consist of means of production, raw materials and labor power. Tools, machines and factories etc. are the means of production. The skills, knowledge, experience and other human faculties used in any kind of work can be considered as labor power. The productive forces represent the capabilities and facilities of a society at its command to enable material production. Relations of production regulate the productive forces, relate the work force with production process and link their output with society at large. The contribution or participation of forces of production in the production process and the manner of linking or relating their output with society constitute the economic mode of a historical stage. If the dialectical components of the base maintain complementary relations, the economic mode of production experiences equilibrium not only within itself but also with its superstructures. Such a situation helps the progress and sustenance of that historical epoch. If the dialectical polemics disturb the symmetry within the base, the resulting imbalance continues until the emergence of a higher form of reconciliation. In each balanced stage of development or epoch of history, the relations of production correspond to the forces of production. "The hand mill gives you society with the feudal lord, the steam mill, society with the industrial capitalist."[41] Feudal relations of production existed because they fostered the development of productive forces of feudal times. They restricted the mobility of the serfs and the workers, and tied them to land or to manufacturing units. With the development of science and technology, forces of production were revolutionized with the invention of machines. The steam mill replaced the hand mill. Laborers in large numbers were required for the maximum use of steam powered machines in large factories. The peasants and workers of the feudal farmland began to move to cities to join in the industrial army. Feudal relations of production were not powerful enough to control and regulate the revolutionized forces of production and their attraction of workers. Yet the feudal lords continued to restrict the mobility of workers to be challenged by the capitalists with the support of workers. They fought against the feudal system and overthrew it and established the capitalist mode of production. The relation between lord and serf was replaced with the relation between capitalist and wage laborers. The emerged forces and relations of production constituted the economic structure of capitalism, on which rose capitalist superstructures with new forms of state, legal system, religion and morality.

    Marx summarized the discussion: "The general result at which I arrived and which, once won, served as a guiding thread for my studies, can be briefly formulated as follows: In the social production of their life, men enter into definite relations that are indispensable and independent of their will, relations of production which correspond to a definite stage of development of their material productive forces. The sum total of these relations of production constitutes the economic structure of society, the real foundation, on which rises a legal and political superstructure and to which correspond definite forms of social consciousness. The mode of production of material life conditions the social, political and intellectual life process in general. It is not the consciousness of men that determines their being, but, on the contrary, their social being that determines their consciousness. At a certain stage of their development, the material productive forces of society come in conflict with the existing relations of production, or-what is but a legal expression for the same thing- with the property relations within which they have been at work hitherto. From forms of development of the productive forces these relations turn into their fetters. Then, begins an epoch of social revolution. With the change of the economic foundation the entire immense superstructure is more or less rapidly transformed. In considering such transformations a distinction should always be made between the material transformation of the economic conditions of production, which can be determined with the precision of natural science, and the legal, political, religious, aesthetic or philosophic-in short, ideological forms in which men become conscious of this conflict and fight it out."[42] If we simplify the Marxian concept of social change, we can say that it is a three-step process. Development in the forces of production changes the relations of production and they together as the base formulate the superstructures.

Science and technology are rapidly revolutionizing the production process and every leap is a step towards substituting human hand with robotic hand. Artificial intelligence streamlines and corrects human intelligence. There may come a time when all human work may be substituted with machines having artificial intelligence. At that time, human activities at the economic base, superstructural relations and the theory of social revolutions may have to be understood or interpreted differently. Dialectics is the ever occurring and never recurring trajectory of changing resemblances. Human intelligence has to intervene and human hand has to interact. Otherwise, humans will be estranged in an antagonistic society divided between robots and humans.

CHAPTER 8
DIALECTICAL LOGIC OF SUCCESSIVE STAGES OF HISTORY

Since 1849 Marx had been living in London and mostly pondering over the economic theories and developments. He spent much of his time in the British Museum reading economic classics and collecting economic and commercial data for writing mostly the books on political economy. In the process *A Contribution to the Critique of Political Economy* and its *Preface* were written in 1859. Later its parts were incorporated in *Capital* published in 1867. *Preface to A Contribution to the Critique of Political Economy* became very important document to the study of historical materialist understanding of social formation. It pronounces the dialectics existing at the economic base and also between base and superstructures. Marx formulated a historiography of developmental and dialectical trajectory through successive stages as was observed by him in the European history. He noticed that the revolutionary social transformation of any epoch had first begun with revolutionary change in the forces of production mostly due to quantitative leap in the availability of raw materials or free labor or a qualitative upgrading of instruments of production. The revolutionary leap in the forces of production disturbed the conventional relations of production that had initially resisted to accommodate the revolutionized facilities of enhanced forces of production but to be withered away in the current of change. The first victim of the process was the rigid political dominance that was the backbone of the conventional and obsolete relations of production. The birth of new political superstructure with a tendency to accept new relations of production would be effective in linking the process of production, distribution and consumption suitably with society. Along with the changes in the base structure, all superstructures would experience radical transformation. That was the way Marx was describing the birth of a new historical epoch. Accordingly he interpreted successive stages of history as constituted by different modes of production, "In broad outlines Asiatic, ancient, feudal and modern bourgeois modes of production can be designated as progressive epochs in the economic formation of society."[43] Hence, dialectical conflict within the economic base between forces of production and relations of production reaches a synthesis or reconciliation in the new economic mode that conditions the superstructures that are in agreement with the emerged base and also advantageous to one another.

Marx and Engels portrayed primitive communism as the initial stage of history. There was no class division, because there was no individual ownership of property. "Production at all former stages of society was essentially collective and likewise consumption took place by the direct distribution of the products within larger or smaller communistic communities."[44] Engels described two types of primeval classless communities. One was a community of noble savages who lived on hunting. All members of the tribe were willing to exert maximum of their effort for the fulfilment of the basic needs of all. Some among them who were smart enough to possess landed property for cultivation converted others as agricultural laborers. The hunting band was divided to warring groups. The new owners of land tried to oppress them for the perpetuation of exploitation. Along with the above change, cultural habits also were changed and the movement of workers was restricted and they were bound to land.

Another type of communistic community was the non-polarized farming community who had retained their original communal life through common ownership of land, cultivating their farm in common. As in the cases of tribal groups, all able persons of the community, without competing one another, labored to procure what was needed for all. As the primitive hunters, communal farmers also enjoyed tilling and harvesting collectively.[45]

The ancient imperialists converted the common property

relations into the properties of elite families. Some of them established slavery especially in the conquered lands. Slaves were there in many parts of post tribal societies, mostly as domestic slaves. But slavery can be considered as a mode of production only when the production was entirely done by slaves. That time slaves were purchased by property owners like oxen has been bought by farmers from cattle market. The payment was done only once, and not to the slave but to the slave merchant. They were resold as commodities with resale value.[46] They were tied to the land and forcefully expropriated their work with no mercy on them. And they were fed not for survival but to extract more work.

Entitlement of property for some and estrangement of property for others destroyed primitive communism and that was the beginning of continuous tension and conflict within society. During the primitive communism, work was not only a productive force for the satisfaction of basic needs but also a life realizing natural act of enjoyment. For example, hunting and fishing were means of livelihood and also acts of thrill and enjoyment. It was the same with agriculture as well. In an antagonistic society, work was not a pleasurable act. In the heart of heart workers resisted to work while working in the masters' farm. On the contrary masters enforced work by placing supervisors above them. Punishment and torture appeared as necessary components of enforced work. Labor, the natural and necessary human quality, became the least desired and unpleasant human act.

With the origin of class distinctions in relations to human interaction with property, the primitive ways of linking the product of human labor with society also was revolutionized. All the products were not to be shared by all. The slaves or workers contributed their maximum and received the minimum that was just enough for their subsistence. Owners of property enjoyed the maximum. Class division on the basis of division of labor created disparity on the enjoyment of fruits of labor by discriminating the least accessed as the last in the society and maintained suitable conditions for the perpetuation of exploitation. The minority cannot keep the vast majority under their control unless they apply direct or indirect force on them. Hence, state as the first among the ideological superstructures was born to protect the interests of the propertied class. State maintained law and order in a conflict situation to the advantage of the advantaged.[47]

Though primitive communism had only limited facilities, it was not nasty. Engels treated it as a beautiful social system that could be emulated. Therefore, the progressive evolution of society should end in the establishment of a society with primitive communitarian attitude with modern facilities. The epochal transition of society from the primitive communism to the modern communism may be stated as the evolution of property relations from communal property to common property with all the advantages of capitalist forces of production: a higher form of communal property. Until the private property is annihilated and classless society is established, property for all is a better option as suggested by other socialists. Communism under the formative process may have to accept some of the socialist or welfare capitalist programs and plans for ensuring necessary welfare and minimum comfort of the people.

Asiatic mode of production may be referred to the agricultural economy of Asia and North Africa and comparable with the ancient mode of production of European model. Cultivation of common property by the community mostly for the use of the members was the simplest form of property relations in Asian countries. A surplus was distributed among other communities and a small portion was shared with the state as tax. In a complex economy, agriculture was aligned with handicrafts and the work was carried out by the groups bound by the unalterable division of labor. It was a reference to caste system. In parts of Asia land was distributed among farmers by king or state and the rent was collected from farmers. Permanent individual holding also was entitled. In some areas, the absolute monarch was the owner of the land and the vast majority of workers produced for the people of palaces and temples. The surplus was used for the construction of monuments propagating the might of the emperors.[48]

The next in the successive epoch of European history was feudalism. It established social, political and economic obligations among different classes through the distribution of landed property. The obligations were mutual but graded within the hierarchically structured society. Marx and Engels had scarcely dealt with the origin of feudalism from the womb of ancient mode or slave mode of production. From the days of primitive communism to the collapse of feudalism, agriculture was the major economic activity and the difference among the successive stages of agricultural societies was determined by the manner of holding landed property and the relation of farm workers with the land and land owners. Therefore, the revolutionary gap of one to the other stage was not so different to be explicitly visible. The difference of one agricultural stage from the other agricultural stage was mostly decided by the tillers' relation with property and the mode of distribution of agricultural output with the exploiters, the exploited and also with the members of all other classes. Under the slave mode of agricultural production, workers did not have any claim over the cultivable land. Peasants' relation to property was revolutionary which was mostly attributed to the political changes in the Roman Empire in the Middle Ages. With the dominance of German tribes in the Roman Empire, German primitive mode of production was synthesized with Roman mode of production. Roman citizens who had been tortured and usurped by their bureaucrats were liberated by German tribes. The liberated Romans agreed to divide a portion of land among themselves by lot under the condition of keeping a large segment of property undivided for common use according to the gentile constitution. There were also free farmers in Germany and France. They were also doing common service and also military service in need. Frequent wars and plunders weakened the communities holding common property and also of free farmers. The victorious kings and military leaders forcefully appropriated the property to be divided among their magnates and servitors in return of their military service and share of tax.

Feudal order slowly emerged from it in medieval Europe. It was a hierarchically arranged political jurisdiction over land as the major economic source with political bindings. The monarch or the dominant king distributed land among peasants through landlords and in return their military service was ensured. Landlords were empowered with administrative and judicial powers over the people of their land.[49] Under feudalism peasants were tied to the land and even inherited it. Peasants did not have the mobility that the slaves had. Mobility of salves was not for their good, but only to be sold in the market to be suffered miserably under another master. The perceptible progress of feudalism from slave mode was the possession of means of production and products by the peasants. They also enjoyed a kind social recognition within the community. But it is difficult to attribute to a revolution in the forces of production as the cause for the origin of feudalism in Europe.

Marx and Engels, in many of their books, dealt with the breakdown of feudalism due to the occurrence of revolution first in the forces of production to the emergence of industrial capitalism with liberal market system as its relations of production. Whereas other thinkers attributed the cause of the collapse of feudalism and the rise of capitalism to frequent wars, emergence of nation states, and change in the market conditions etc., Marx and Engels observed that the advancement in the production technology with the invention of gigantic machineries and the entry of courageous entrepreneurs ready to invest in them for the establishment of huge factories for the massive production and multiplication of profit as the cause of revolutionary change of European society from feudalism to capitalism.

Capitalism is one of the most vibrant epochs that the world history has ever seen. It has been constantly undergoing rapid developments. The process began with the conversion of mercantile capitalism into industrial capitalism. Marx and Engels narrated the emergence and revolutionary growth of capitalism in the *Manifesto of the Communist Party* in lucid and impressive manner. Merchants, originally the serfs of the Middle Ages, from the Western and Central Europe had begun trade with the Eastern Europe and became very rich. They sold agricultural implements, other tools and goods from the manufacturing units of the West in the East and procured food grains from the Eastern farmlands for feeding the populated cities of the West. Similarly, ship and boat making for the Mediterranean navigation made the Italian middle class rich. Money making was a very thrilling exercise for them and ventured into new areas of burgeoning wealth. They encouraged navigation for finding less expensive sea routes, new and cheap raw materials and establishing global trade centers. They standardized currency and gained universal acceptance. The simultaneous revolutionary development of science and technology was openly accepted and aptly used by the emerging middle class. They established huge factories, employed large number of workers, loaned kings and lords and finally became the lord of the world. *Manifesto* announces the arrival of the bourgeois as, "Meantime the markets kept ever growing, the demand ever rising. Even manufacturer no longer sufficed. Thereupon, steam and machinery revolutionised industrial production. The place of manufacture was taken by the giant, Modern Industry; the place of the industrial middle class by industrial millionaires, the leaders of the whole industrial armies, the modern bourgeois."[50] The social, cultural and economic regulations of the guilds in the cities and feudalism in the villages were broken and unbound the peasants from feudal fetters. Along with free movement, they demanded participation in government and ensured free speech. Modern agriculture, industry, transport, commerce, communication and so on were growing very fast and in the process, the bourgeois was asserting its economic, political and cultural dominance over all other classes and people. New forms of oppression and exploitation were systematically and legally incorporated into the system. Hence, the modern bourgeois travelled on a long path of development, "of a series of revolutions in the modes of production and exchange."[51] With their adventurous effort the modern bourgeois created an economic base by themselves and given to all who have purchasing power, and on that base, they constructed democratic republic to freely speak their will as the will of all.

While the Manifesto describes the materialist conditions of the origin of capitalist mode of production, *Socialism: Utopian and Scientific* deals with the impact of cultural, intellectual and political struggles of the period on the rise of bourgeois as a class from the womb of feudalism. In its emergence from feudal clutches, the bourgeois had to reckon with the Roman Catholic Church that Engels had identified as the international center of feudalism. The Church had united the divided feudal Western Europe, preserved its traditions and political system. Church organized itself on the feudal hierarchical model and occupied one third of the landed property of the Catholic world. In the fight against the feudal network that had been politically, culturally and economically centralized and organized, the middle class was inspired by modern intellectual developments and strengthened by the rise of science. The new science, intellectual enlightenment and materialism challenged the intellectual vacuum, scientific ignorance and false pretentions of the Church. The bourgeois supported the findings and inventions of new science and joined hand with enlightened intellectuals against the temporal and spiritual feudal lords and their mass peasant bases of the countries. According to Engels "The long fight of the bourgeoisie against feudalism culminated in three great, decisive battles" such as the Protestant Reformation of Luther and Calvin in Western Europe, the democratic struggles by the Protestant bourgeoisie along with peasant yeomanry against monarchy and the aristocracy in England and the antireligious and antimonarchical Great French Revolution.[52] They created favorable situations to the economically advantageous bourgeoisie to do away with feudalism along with its tradition and culture. The cultural and political supplements added by Engels to the economic formation of the bourgeois society shows that the superstructures also play important role in the social formation. But their impact on the formation of a new epoch would have been meagre or nil if the feudal economic conditions were not revolutionized. It would have ended in the mere change of rulers or boundaries.

Marx and Engels foresaw the birth of communism at the culmination of capitalism. It would happen when capitalism collapses due to its unbearable burden of its own making. Capitalism persists with irreconcilable contradictions within it. It is driven by competitive spirit and exploitative tendencies decorated with bourgeois values of liberty, equality and fraternity. Each capitalist has to compete with every other capitalist for survival. Profit alone is the guiding principle. Bourgeois humanism discovers human innovative capabilities and converts them into mere instruments of production of marketable commodities. "It (capitalism) has resolved personal worth into exchange value, and in place of the numberless indefeasible chartered freedoms, has set up that single, unconscionable freedom - Free Trade. In one word, for exploitation, veiled by religious and political illusions, it has substituted naked, shameless, direct, brutal exploitation."[53] In earlier epochs what were considered as evil or bad, had been practiced in a hidden manner. But capitalism treats the so-called evils as necessary conditions for the effective functioning of capitalist system and therefore, most of them are silently approved and some of them are practiced openly. Marx illustrated dichotomous and suspicious attitude of Birmingham bourgeois caused by the excess competition. They were compelled to indulge in foul means as employers that they otherwise be ashamed of doing.[54] The bourgeois struggled to keep up the moral worthiness according to its standards but were compelled to practice fraudulent means to be successful as capitalist.

Technology is the constructive and destructive source of capitalism. Fast changing technology rapidly upgrades capitalist means of production and no capitalist can remain as a capitalist without installing instruments with developed technology. As a follow up to the advancement of technology, quality of product is improved and quantity increased to the elimination of surplus workers and docile capitalists. Workers compete among themselves by updating with their skills to cope with technological changes and retain a place in the shrinking employment market. Restless capitalists unceasingly modify instruments of production and persuasively expand market to retain a place among the monopoly capitalists. Ever growing forces of production and expanding market reach the situation of saturation on the one hand and on the other hand stagnation in the movement of raw materials and finished commodities. A reversal of growth begins and system declines. Capitalism falls into a vicious circle of over production, less consumption, lockdown of companies, unemployment and they will be followed by recession and economic depression and further deterioration of social conditions of living. This can be treated as a mature time to convert capitalist system into communism. Labor being the transformative power within the forces of production was empowered by Marx and Engels with revolutionary power. In their effort to stand with the exploited workers, they lost accession to their inheritance and reputed status in the intellectual circle of that time. Marx did not enjoy comfortable family life and his personal loss was very painful. Among the seven children, four died at very young age in London mostly because of their poor living conditions. From 1842 to 1883, from Paris to his graveyard, Engels accompanied Marx as a real comrade for encouraging and uniting the workers of the world to challenge and overthrow the bourgeois political dominance and taking control over the state administration to regulate economic base and alter it suitably to the building up of a social system that can look after the welfare of all.

    The proletarians after gaining political power, should work steadily and consciously for the emancipation of humankind. The dictatorship of the proletariat transforms the collapsed capitalist society into communism with the optimum utilization of advanced capitalist facilities but by removing the capitalist habits from human practices. It reconstructs the society by gradually purging the bourgeois inclination of profit making and the proletarian habit of expecting reward for their contribution during the period of social revolution. Dictatorship of the proletariat gradually cleanses the weeds of the previous society and selectively incorporates its strength for the formation of communist society. It is identified as the socialist period of the communism that is in the course of making. It collectively plans and commonly implements its programs for the integral development of the individual and society. The process continues till the abolition of private property and the establishment of the socialized character of the means of production. Thus, communism eliminates class division and class-based exploitation. But classless society can survive only in a stateless atmosphere. Otherwise, the states opposed to communism may work against the classless self-governed and decentralized communes and destroy their existence by tactically encroaching into their domain and forcefully attaching them with dominant nation states

CHAPTER 9
IRON LAW OF CAPITALIST DIALECTICS

In the previous chapter, we dealt with the successive stages of history as driven by causal dialectics within economic base and between base and superstructures. Among the successive stages of European history, they elaborately dealt with the epochal transformation from feudalism to capitalism and finally predicted the birth of communism from the womb of capitalism. The scientific rigor that was attributed to the historical occurrence by Marx mislead communist theory of revolution with ambiguous interpretations.

Qualitative changes in human life and society, quantitative leap in the capitalist mode of production, stages of capitalist accumulation and its inevitable collapse due to its own excess are the major themes of the *Capital*. The capitalist mode of production destroyed independent labor, created socialization of labor and increased its efficiency through division of labor. The socialized and dependent labor became the instruments of accumulation for the capitalists through the appropriation of the surplus labor. Capitalists who were condemned to be free to be driven by the market conditions, reinvested the accumulated wealth to the new domains of expanding economy to exist as capitalists. The tendency of capitalist accumulation expedited competition among the expropriators with the urge to annihilate competitive compatriots and monopolize the production process and exploit the choiceless conditions of market.

Success is not always in favor of the successful alone. With stress and suspicion, capitalists flourish or decline. If they decline, the process of declining continues as an ongoing war, fighting for success till the total collapse. The first victims of the monopolistic capitalism are fellow bourgeoisies and the worst victims are the workers, but always disgruntled are the consumers with declining bargaining power. The prime values of liberal society such as liberty, happiness, harmonious and egalitarian living are in danger. All become victims of the vicious accumulation of capital.

The capitalist tendency of unending urge for profit making and enthusiastic entry of individuals into expanding capitalism react opposite to monopolistic tendency of capitalism. The hype of prosperity in an imaginary invisible market attracts more aspiring capitalists to invest in production process and fill the market beyond the purchasing power. The process ends in the cumulating of market with abundant products much above the human inclination to consume or waste. Immobile commodities and services downgrade the economy, and the producers meet with heavy loss and close down the companies leading to unemployment and poverty especially among the workers and cause "the mass of misery, oppression, slavery, degradation, exploitation; but with this too grows the revolt of the working-class, a class always increasing in numbers, and disciplined, united, organised by the very mechanism of the process of capitalist production itself. The monopoly of capital becomes a fetter upon the mode of production, which has sprung up and flourished along with, and under it. Centralisation of the means of production and socialisation of labour at last reach a point where they become incompatible with their capitalist integument. Thus, integument is burst asunder. The knell of capitalist private property sounds. The expropriators are expropriated."[55]   At the ripe time, workers of the world have to unite and save humanity from the evils of capitalist accumulation. Marx, in his "Preface to the first German Edition" of the first volume of Capital, predicted that it was natural for the industrially advanced England to move to its next stage as dictated by the iron laws of nature, because capitalist mode of production expanded extensively in England with maximum number of disturbed workers.[56]

Marx and Engels analyzed bourgeois society and observed the signs of inner contradictions and systemic failures within capitalist countries. The favoring factors of a revolution were present in the advanced capitalist countries such as the presence of a large number of discontented wage laborers, unredeemable crises within capitalism, and sufficiently developed instruments of production for the creation of future communist society. Considering the above parameters, the most developed England was the country most inclined to undergo communist revolution. Marx was very much aware of the unpreparedness of English workers and advised the party to develop organizational strategies, "The English have all the *material* necessary for the social revolution. What they lack is *the spirit of generalization and revolutionary fervour*. Only the General Council can provide them with this, can thus accelerate the truly revolutionary movement here, and in consequence, *everywhere*."[57] On the contrary, the proletariat of the industrial society did not develop the revolutionary spirit consistently. They were not diverted from the revolutionary goal by the bourgeois strategies and national sentiments. The trigger of workers' anger ended in wars between nations and denigrated the spirit of international communism. They had fallen into the trap of narrow patriotism. Thus, the crisis of capitalism assumed perverted political forms and ended in international disasters.

According to the iron laws of nature, the higher stage in social evolution is born from the womb of its decayed lower stage as a sprout from the seed. In the evolutionary process, communism will emerge from capitalism as a resolution to the capitalist conflicts. According to historical materialism, the revolutionary transformation begins with the irreconcilable contradiction in the economic base between its forces of production and relations of production. Revolutionized forces of production replace the irrelevant relations of production of that period with new relations of production according to their suitability. In response to the changes in the economic base all superstructures are transformed. A new historic epoch is emerged consisting of newly formed base and superstructures. With the maturing of economic base, the then superstructures are changed, resulting in the transformation of whole society. Accordingly, Marx predicted the emergence of communism after capitalism. Many Marxists began to understand the history of successive modes of production as universal, uniform, single-linear and progressive. But the historical evidence did not witness the historical materialist natural law working with iron necessity. No serious communist revolution happened in the most advanced England. In other advanced industrial European countries, workers' revolutions were suppressed on the streets. The unpredictability and contradictory consequences of the scientific law disillusioned the optimism of the communists and roused celebrations in the capitalist camps. The historical materialist historiography was declared unscientific and imaginary by the antagonists.

Marx and Engels studied different branches knowledge not to acquire proficiency in those areas but to show how human society had been maintaining oppression and exploitation for economic advantage, and how all superstructures including different branches of knowledge had been favoring the continuation of oppression and exploitation. Engels later admitted that the causal determination was unexpected and over-emphasized. According to them the `base-superstructure' image was not a one-way relationship but a reciprocal one. The economic base determines the superstructures and the superstructures influence the economic base in their own way. As there were misunderstandings in the economic formation of history, Engels clarified it in his letter to W. Borgius on 25, January 1894. "Political, juridical, philosophical, religious, literary, artistic, etc., development is based on economic development. But all these react upon one another and also upon the economic basis. It is not that the economic situation is the cause, solely active, while everything else is only passive in effect." Engels continues to assert the human intervention in history, "...it is not,... that the economic situation produces an automatic effect. No. Men make their history themselves, only they do so in a given environment, which conditions it, and on the basis of actual relations already existing, among which the economic relations,... are still ultimately the decisive ones,..."[58] When people are chained with any theory, they become dogmatic. Proletarian or revolutionaries' intervention is necessary for social transformation. According to historical materialism, the basis or the most fundamental of all human development was historical human interaction with nature. "Men make their own history, but they do not make it just as they please; they do not make it under circumstances chosen by themselves, but under circumstances directly encountered, given and transmitted from the past."[59] This shows how Marx incorporated the humanistic principle i.e., `Man makes himself' into his historical materialism. The creative possibility of human beings was not without any limit, but determined by the historical conditions. Unfortunately, workers who really interacted with nature were forgotten in history. While the workers who constituted the real force that had been changing the world were not recognized, the spectators were honored as architects of transformation, and gained right over the real creators of history to be exploited. The exploiters were projected as the great carriers of the movements of history. In order to assert the significance of the working class above the bourgeois class, Marx and Engels emphasized the causal dialectics of the economic base.

A less deterministic version of the `base-superstructure' image does not mean that it was unimportant in Marxism. It was the main principle, and the root cause of any revolutionary change. A less deterministic view of dialectics of economic contradictions as the primary cause of radical social transformation is not substituted with any superstructures. Superstructures play relevant roles in transforming or in retaining an epoch. But they are considered as secondary causes moving in consonant with their economic interests. Marx and Engels emphasized the importance of political revolution for the establishment of socialist society. If thought and politics did not have any causal significance, the intellectual and political efforts of Marx and Engels would have gone in vain. Thus, "In considering such transformations a distinction should always be made between the material transformation of the economic conditions of production, which can be determined with the precision of natural science, and the legal, political, religious, aesthetic or philosophic – in short, ideological forms in which men become conscious of this conflict and fight it out".[60] In order to seek a communist society, it was not the tool that had to be revolutionized but the one who handled the tools. Workers handled tools to deal with materials effectively and change them for the welfare of all. And the real transformer of the material things was considered as the proper person to transform the society also. The non-analytical communists interpreted the dialectical contradictions within the economic base as the sole cause of revolutionary processes and equated it with natural phenomena and consequently, they anticipated the establishment of a communist society as the culmination of antagonistic capitalism. Birth, growth and decay are natural phenomena. But we are not allowing them to occur as they take place. We choose to intervene and alter as much as the biological conditions agree. Human intervention is a natural process. At the ripening of right time of revolution, the revolutionaries have to do their natural function. Marx identified the proletariat as the bearers of revolution who have to convert the decayed capitalism into communism, as it is the workers who are transforming society by their hard toil. The proletarians have been updating their tool handling skill and operating the revolutionized capitalist means of production efficiently. Capitalist means of production were sufficient to produce abundantly to satisfy the needs of all. It was the task of proletariat to convert capitalism into communism to use the capitalist facilities for the benefit of all. Thus, Marx and Engels tried to revolutionize proletarians with critical consciousness. For them, it was not the tool that had to be revolutionized but the one who handled the tool. The real transformer of the material things was considered as the proper person to transform society. They tried to make the laborers realize their historical role for bringing about the social revolution. The proletariat was advised to wait for the appropriate time of the decay of capitalism and then abolish it fully and completely with a view to establish communism.

After the Russian revolution in 1917, the possibility of successive epochs was debated not only among the Marxists but also among the capitalists. The socialist parties of the advanced Europe expected that socialist revolution would occur first in their countries where proletarians were in majority. While the uprisings in those countries were suppressed, a less developed agrarian Russia marched ahead with political revolution successfully towards the establishment of communism. Thus, the first communist country was born much before its productive forces for which there was room in it had not been developed and higher relations of production appeared before the material conditions of their existence had not matured in the womb of the old society. Therefore, the revolutionary task arose before the material conditions for its solution was neither in existence nor were in the process of formation.[61] Marx and Engels gave different theoretical framework for different countries. Historical materialism very clearly explains that the theory should be context depended. Regarding Russian path to revolution, Marx suggested different scheme for revolution. In 1861, there was a move by the Russian authorities to convert the collective peasant communes' production method into the capitalist mode of production. Towards that end the Russian state privatized the land and the other properties. Marx warned the socialists about its dangers. "If Russia continues to advance along the path she has followed since 1861, she will miss the best chance history has ever offered a people, and will have to undergo all the fatal vicissitudes of the capitalist system."[62] If the peasant commune was destroyed, he feared that the peasants who were driven out of their land would undergo severe misery. Above all, the commune which was collective in nature was a strong base for the socialist society. If it was destroyed by capitalism, it would be very difficult to establish a socialist society in an agrarian state. Therefore, he asserted the need for a Russian revolution to save the Russian Commune even though the forces of production were not fully mature. Following the line of Marx, Engels encouraged peasant revolt against the oppressive state which was planning to annihilate the collective farming of the small peasants for the sake of bourgeois farming. "...: if anything of this community is to be salvaged, the first requirement is the overthrow of the tsarist despotism, a revolution in Russia."[63] And Marx and Engels expected that the bourgeois means of production could be developed in the post-revolutionary society with the assistance of proletariat of the advanced countries.

Though Marx and Engels hoped a revolution in Western Europe as the starting point for communist development, they encouraged political revolution even before the economic conditions were mature, if the bearers of revolution had sufficiently grown with the critical consciousness for political praxis. This alternative pattern was suggested mainly for the agrarian states as the destruction of peasant communities would throw the ordinary people to be massively exploited by the ruling class as well as the emerging bourgeoisies. By that time, if a socialist government is established in such an agrarian society, it can develop the capitalist instruments of production for the advantage of all, with collective efforts.

CHAPTER 10
DIALECTICS BETWEEN STATE AND CIVIL SOCIETY

Conversion of communal society into political society has been debated and resisted at different stages of political history. But privileged or structured political establishments emerged and regulated or reorganized social relations, customs and social ethos. Ardent desire for collective communal society is sentimentally attributed on nation states and made them dominant political establishments.

Hegel to Marx

Hegel conceived state as the highest manifestation of Spirit that appeared for solving conflicts in civil society. The state was destined to establish social order. Once, social institutions were organically united and functioned as a totality in the society. Hence, social behavior was harmonious and peaceful. Individuals socialized in and through family and associations. Bond of love unified the members of a family. Members of an association were united by the specific task or purpose to be fulfilled by the association in civil society. Associations were formed mainly to perform economic activities. Members joined in any association for making personal gain while fulfilling social and material needs of civil society. The inner conflict between individual ambition and common good was reflected in social relations, negating one another, and disturbing social cohesion and organic unity of civil society. State originated as an external necessity of civil society, a superior authority capable of solving unresolvable conflicts that disturbed the interdependent social and material relations in civil society. Marx remarks sarcastically about it,

"The state arises from them in an unconscious and arbitrary fashion, the family and civil society appear as the dark natural ground from which the light of the state arises."[64] Accordingly, the higher wisdom of state subjugated dichotomies of social and material relations in civil society, and made the conflicting civil laws subordinate to the state laws. Thus, state imposed its means on civil society for the creation of peace and order.[65] But, Marx critically located the state as the alienation of civil society. State in any form, destroys the communal nature of society, divides it and favors the dominant group against the subjugated groups. Hence, state is not actually resolving conflicts in civil society but siding with the beneficiaries of conflict. State emerged as an organ of oppression for the continuation of conflict on behalf of the propertied upper class to oppress the propertyless to the advantage of the propertied. "The antithesis of state and civil society is thus fixed: the state does not reside in, but outside civil society."[66] State exists only as an organ of coercion, enforcing power against all others. Among them the least advantaged are open to maximum oppression and exploitation.

The concept of alienation was an important theme of early Marx. In the beginning, he used it to attack religion. Later he discovered the estrangement in political establishments and economic systems. The attributes of God are the alienated human qualities and abilities projected in an imaginary reality. The real creator becomes insignificant and the created acts as the creator. Workers, the real producers of commodities, are estranged from production process, reversely in proportion to their contribution. On the contrary, the non-producers are acquiring name, fame and profit. Family and civil society, the real domains of social relations and material interactions, are abstracted and subjugated as appendages to the abstracted idea called state. The alienated roles of civil society in the areas of social relations are attributed to state. Henceforth, the abstracted entity is taking in its hand the powers of controlling social and material relations. The estranged existence of civil society empowers the ideal state as real and necessary institution. Consequently, the ruling elite who are enlightened with the highest consciousness and wisdom of the manifested spirit of Hegelian philosophy, entitled themselves with the legitimacy to rule over the citizens and supervise social relations and institutions. Communal ethos and collective decision procedures are substituted by police, judiciary and bureaucracy. Marx considered bureaucracy as the most oppressive apparatus of the state functioning as the "civil society of the state" and confronted the "state of civil society."[67] The duty of bureaucrats is to formalize the will of the monarch as the will of civil society and deify it above the so-called trivialities of civil society. In the process, bureaucracy grew as an exploitative institution, because "The bureaucracy has the state, the spiritual essence of society, in its possession, as its *private property*."[68]

A detailed treatment on the origin of state is dealt by Engels in *The Origin of the Family, Private Property and the State*. It is one of the last classics of Marx and Engels duo. The book is a unique work from the perspectives of Marxian anthropology. Marx was instrumental in inducing Engels to write this book. After the death of Marx, Engels made meticulous effort to complete his intellectual projects. In this regard the notable achievement of Engels was the editing and publishing of the second and the third volumes of *Capital*. While searching the manuscripts, he discovered Marx's Abstract of Morgan's "Ancient Society". Lewis H. Morgan was an American anthropologist. Morgan provided insights into the existence of primitive communism and the materialist understanding of social evolution. Marx realized that the social living was a natural inclination for human beings. It motivated Engels to make a thorough study on the materialist conditioning of the origin of social institutions that led to the writing of *The Origin of the Family, Private Property and the State*. It justified the possibility of stateless and classless communes that were prevalent one time in the history.

The Origin of the Family, Private Property and the State analyzed the history of disintegration of primitive-communal system and the emergence of state administration as the outcome of the formation of classes based on private property. For example, Engels attributed the cause of the decay of the gentile system of the Grecian gens to the "father right and the inheritance of property by the children."[69] The families that accumulated wealth dictated their terms on gens, grew themselves as the leaders of the community and established hereditary nobility or monarchy to rule over their own tribes. They enslaved the members of their own tribes for the accumulation of wealth in land and conducted systematic raids to capture cattle and slaves and to plunder treasure in the process of expanding their wealth. "Only one thing was missing: an institution that would not only safeguard the newly-acquired property of private individuals against the communistic traditions of the gentile order, ... an institution that would perpetuate, not only the newly-rising class division of society, but also the right of the possessing class to exploit the non-possessing classes and the rule of the former over the latter. And this institution arrived. The *state* was invented."[70] Hence, state should not be considered as an external necessity but imposed from within civil society.

Ideological Functions of State

In the *Manifesto*, Marx and Engels identified the selective operations of state in civil society in favor of upper class, promoting its interests for oppressing all dissenting voices or differentiating value systems. "Political power, properly so called, is merely the organised power of one class for oppressing another."[71] State is an organ of coercion restricting any trespassing by the subjugated into the domains of the dominant. Hence, state cannot be treated as an external necessity that reconciles conflicts in the social and material relations within civil society, but only as an apparatus of organized oppression. It is not the resolution but the continuation of organized conflict. State represents the will of the owners of wealth, creating favorable conditions of accumulation and providing protection for the abuse of commonwealth in the name of common good. Standing army, bureaucracy and police are the visible faces of state that are venerated, respected and served by the oppressed.

There are many mysteries about human relations that are experienced but not understood. The most pathetic one among them is the oppression at the will of the oppressed and the exploitation at the request of the exploited. They accept the conditions of oppression and exploitation as unavoidable or best of all possible options. Marx and Engels observed the phenomena differently. According to them the conditions of oppression and exploitation were constructed and favorable attitude and circumstances were created. "The class which has the means of material production at its disposal, consequently also controls the means of mental production, so that the ideas of those who lack the means of mental production are on the whole are subject to it. The ruling ideas are nothing more than the ideal expression of the dominant material relations, the dominant material relations grasped as ideas: hence of the relations which make the one class the ruling one, therefore, the ideas of its dominance." [72] Class of rulers exists only in a divided society. Perpetuation of ideas perpetuates them as natural and therefore acceptable and legal.

Conflict within the Dominant Class

The ruling class and the propertied class were not always existed with one mind and one body. At the beginning of the bourgeois era, state engaged in protecting private property from trespassing, and at the same time, it promoted its own interest to the extent of displeasing the owners of property, especially on the question of mode of sharing profit. The collection of tithe and tax disturbed their social cohesion. Thus, state while reconciliating with property owners acted against them, and the gap increased between the political power and economic dominance. The modern political history was the history of eventful emergence and growth of the bourgeois and its ideologies against the traditional rulers and conventions. "Each step in the development of the bourgeoisie was accompanied by a corresponding political advance of that class. An oppressed class under the sway of the feudal nobility,..., afterwards, in the period of manufacture proper, serving either the semi-feudal or the absolute monarchy as a counterpoise against the nobility, and, in fact, corner-stone of the great monarchies in general, the bourgeoisie has at last, since the establishment of Modern Industry and of the world-market, conquered for itself, in the modern representative State, exclusive political sway. The executive of the modern State is but a committee for managing the common affairs of the whole bourgeoisie."[73] Thus, the ruling class and the propertied class found synthesis under bourgeois democracy. The monarchies of modern European nations did not solve the conflict with the emerging bourgeoisie but the impoverishment due to continuous wars compelled them to make peace with the bourgeois to fill coffers. In the capitalist Europe, the conflict between the state interests and the bourgeois interests continued, sometimes hidden and sometimes open, but agreed on promoting their larger interest of exploiting workers and plundering distant lands. The proletariat accompanied the bourgeois in all their ventures for acquiring property as well as power, but deprived of both. Equality and freedom were the human rights only for the more equals.

CHAPTER 11
DIALECTICS OF DICTATORSHIP OF THE PROLETARIAT

Power is the most misused social need, and power against the misused power is a political need. Socialism aims at social order for the welfare of all, and therefore the socialist state is inclined to become dictatorial. Marx welcomed the dictatorial state of the proletariat to annihilate classes and state. The class rule against the rule of the classes is a conscious step towards classless unity.

Revolution

Earning of profit is the only aim of the bourgeois economy. Hence, the bourgeois forces of production cannot create a welfare society, even though it is possible. In order to use the forces of production for the advantage of all, the capitalist relations of production should be changed, and a new type of relations of production should be established. In a short speech made at the London Conference of the International Working Men's Association, Engels made it clear to all revolutionaries who withdrew from political action, "What is the means of achieving it? The only means is political domination of the proletariat. ... Yet revolution is a supreme political act and those who want revolution must also want the means of achieving it, that is, political action, which prepares the ground for revolution and provides the workers with the revolutionary training without which they are sure to become the dupes."[74] Political revolution is a revolutionary step towards the formation of the dictatorship of the proletariat that plans programs and activities to make society classless and stateless. Through the political revolution, the proletariat should achieve the decision making and implementing power, so that they can change the relations of production and convert social system into one that seeks the common interest.

A state in any form, whether liberal or dictatorial, is coercive, and dictatorship is more forceful than liberal democracy. In that case, is it not to have a political system that provides individual freedom preferable? The anarchist philosophers launched a movement for the abolition of state because they thought that state was not only unnecessary but also a harmful political organization and its main purpose were to curb liberty of individuals. Only the abolition of such a state could restore the liberty of the individuals, and the society should be administrated by the self-governing communes. Marx and Engels were against such an adventurism at the initial periods of successful political revolution of the proletariat. They observed that the citizens of the new regime would be affected by capitalist habit of seeking one's own gain instead of common interest. Hence, they have to be motivated and trained to work for the common good. Above all they feared the active presence of enemies of revolution in and around communes. Thus, a benevolent dictatorship of the revolutionaries with proper plan and facilities has to defend revolution and promote revolutionary cause of establishing classless and stateless society. The dictatorship of the proletariat remained as a political organ in order to develop certain measures for the establishment of the higher stage of communism. In the *Critique of the Gotha Programme*, Marx articulated that the final realization of the annihilation of private property was very difficult to achieve at one stroke, because "What we have to deal with here is a communist society, not as it has *developed* on its own foundations, but, on the contrary, just as it *emerges* from capitalist society; which is thus in every respect, economically, morally and intellectually, still stamped with the birth marks of the old society from whose womb it emerges."[75] Therefore, the transformation in the first phase of communism is gradual and painstaking, and in the beginning the means can be despotic. It is, in principle, against the spirit of Marxism, yet necessary.

Dictatorship of the proletariat is a synthesis between private interest and common interest, a journey from divided society to undivided society. It entertains some of the bourgeois practices as workable means for the success of revolution. Engels, in the Introduction to Marx's *The Civil War in France*, stated "...do you want to know what this dictatorship looks like? Look at the Paris Commune. That was the Dictatorship of the Proletariat."[76] The Paris Commune tried to abolish property in land and convert land rent for public purposes. Progressive taxation, abolition of the rights of inheritance, centralization of banking, and nationalization of communication, transport, education, etc. were a few among other measures. Nationalization and expansion of industries, development of agriculture and related industries were under the consideration of the Paris Commune. Conscious attempt to reduce the gap between town and village through the decentralization of industries was encouraged. Skill developing and job-oriented education were planned for all children by the state. Like these models, each dictatorship of the proletariat can consider various methods that are suitable to its situations.

When everybody becomes a worker, and when everything is planned and managed by the workers themselves as an association "in which the free development of each is the condition for the free development of all", the political supremacy of the proletariat as a class vanishes.[77] In that context, the dictatorship of the proletariat is not annihilated, but becomes irrelevant and hence withers away. Collective and participatory communal administration looks after the affairs of all in the community. Hence, "Society, which will reorganise production on the basis of a free and equal association of the producers, will put the whole machinery of state where it will then belong: into the museum of antiquities, by the side of the spinning-wheel and the bronze axe."[78]. When everybody promotes the common interests, the interests of the ruling class as such are not there. "When at last it becomes the real representative of the whole of society, it renders itself unnecessary. ... State interference in social relations becomes, in one domain after another, superfluous, and then dies out of itself; the government of persons is replaced by the administration of things, and by the conduct of processes of production. The state is not "abolished". It dies out."[79] Due to the change of the social conditions, the functions of the state become irrelevant and superfluous. Still there will be public functions. But they will lose their political character. It will be transformed into simple administrative functions of watching over the true interests of the society. Thus, in the second stage, communism establishes a civil society converting all bourgeois facilities for the good of all, where all gain their original power and creative energy.

Base and superstructures of every epoch are dialectically synthesized. They remain in equilibrium with the tendency towards critical polarization waiting for the right conditions to express the contradictions of the equilibrated stage of history. Sprouting of seeds in the ripe time is a process of decay and growth. All structures are subdivided into their substructures existing either as synthesis or as opposites. The dialectical nature of the economic mode of production is illustrated through dialectical components of forces of production and relations of production. The forces of production consist of means of production, raw materials and labor power. Tools, machines and factories etc. are the means of production. The skills, knowledge, experience and other human faculties used in any kind of work can be considered as labor power. The productive forces represent the capabilities and facilities of a society at its command to enable material production. Relations of production regulate the productive forces, relate the work force with production process and link their output with society at large. The contribution or participation of forces of production in the production process and the manner of linking or relating their output with society constitute the economic mode of a historical stage. If the dialectical components of the base maintain complementary relations, the economic mode of production experiences equilibrium not only within itself but also with its superstructures.

Works by Karl Marx and Frederick Engels

1. Capital vol.I, Progress Publishers, Moscow, 1977
2. Collected Works, vol.3, Progress Publishers, Moscow, 1975
3. Collected Works, vol.4, Progress Publishers, Moscow, 1975
4. Collected Works, vol.5, Progress Publishers, Moscow, 1976
5. Collected Works, vol.6, Progress Publishers, Moscow, 1976
6. Selected Works, (in one vol.), Progress Publishers, Moscow, 1970
7. Selected Works, (in three vol.) vol.2, Progress Publishers, Moscow, 1977

---

[1] Frederick Engels, "The Part Played by Labour in the Transition from Ape to Man", in Marx and Engels, *Selected Works*, (in one vol.), Progress Publishers, Moscow, 1970, p.354

[2] Frederick Engels, "The Part Played by Labour in the Transition from Ape to

Man", *Selected Works*, p.355

[3] Perpetual conflict is the path towards perish. Hegelian philosophy is wrongly used to claim that 'the war is for peace'. Vigilance against such universalization itself is a dialectical criticism.

[4] Frederick Engels, "Socialism: Utopian and Scientific", in Marx and Engels, *Selected Works*, Progress Publishers, Moscow, 1970, p.405

[5] Frederick Engels, "Socialism: Utopian and Scientific", *Selected Works*, p.407

[6] It is expressed with curtsey to Heraclitus.

[7] Frederick Engels, "Feuerbach and End of Classical German Philosophy", *Selected Works*, p.591

[8] Frederick Engels, "Feuerbach and End of Classical German Philosophy", *Selected Works*, p.591

[9] Frederick Engels, "Speech at the Graveside of Karl Marx", in Marx and Engels, *Selected Works*, Progress Publishers, Moscow, 1970, p.429

[10] Frederick Engels, "Feuerbach and End of Classical German Philosophy", *Selected Works*, p.592

[11] The above title is given in the Collected Works published from Moscow, but the first English translation bear the title as *Critique of Hegel's Philosophy of Right*.

[12] Karl Marx, "Contribution to the Critique of Hegel's Philosophy of Law", in Marx and Engels, *Collected Works*, vol.3, Progress Publishers, Moscow, 1975, p.11

[13] Karl Marx, "Theses on Feuerbach", *Collected Works*, vol.5, 1976, p.7

[14] Frederick Engels, "Socialism: Utopian and Scientific", *Selected Works*, p.414

[15] The Indian concept of *adhyasa* can be considered here as an analogy. The true nature of *rope* is concealed and it is revealed as a *snake*.

[16] Karl Marx, "Economic and Philosophic Manuscripts of 1844", in Marx and Engels, *Collected Works*, vol.3, Progress Publishers, Moscow, 1975, p.276

[17] Karl Marx, *Capital*, vol.I, Progress Publishers, Moscow, 1977, p.174

[18] Karl Marx, "Economic and Philosophic Manuscripts of 1844", *Collected Works*, vol.3, pp.271-72

[19] Karl Marx, "Economic and Philosophic Manuscripts of 1844", *Collected Works*, vol.3, p.245

[20] Karl Marx, *Capital*, vol.I, p.77

[21] Karl Marx and Frederick Engels, "The German Ideology", in Marx and Engels, *Collected Works*, vol.5, Progress Publishers, Moscow, 1976, p.23

[22] Frederick Engels, "Feuerbach and End of Classical German Philosophy", in Marx and Engels, *Selected Works*, p.618

[23] Karl Marx and Frederick Engels, "Manifesto of the Communist Party", *Selected*

Works, p.49

[24] Karl Marx and Frederick Engels, "The German Ideology", *Collected Works*, vol. 5, p.36

[25] Frederick Engels, Foreword to "Feuerbach and End of Classical German Philosophy", *Selected Works*, p.585

[26] Karl Marx, "Theses on Feuerbach", *Collected Works*, vol. 5, p.5

[27] Karl Marx, "Contribution to the Critique of Hegel's Philosophy of Law: Introduction", *Collected Works*, vol.3, p.177

[28] Karl Marx, "Contribution to the Critique of Hegel's Philosophy of Law: Introduction", *Collected Works*, vol. 3, p. 182

[29] Karl Marx, *Capital* vol.I, Progress Publishers, Moscow, 1977, p.150

[30] Karl Marx, *Capital*, vol.I, pp.711-712

[31] Karl Marx, *Capital*, vol.I, pp.702-712

[32] Karl Marx, *Capital*, vol.I, p.130

[33] Karl Marx, *Capital*, vol.I, p.587 & 706

[34] Karl Marx, *Capital*, vol.I, p.551

[35] Karl Marx, *Capital*, vol.I, p.257

[36] Karl Marx, *Capital*, vol.I, p.151

[37] Frederick Engels, "Socialism: Utopian and Scientific", in Marx and Engels, *Selected Works*, Progress Publishers, Moscow, 1970, p.376

[38] Frederick Engels, "Socialism: Utopian and Scientific", *Selected Works*, p.411

[39] Karl Marx, "Preface to a Contribution to the Critique of Political Economy", *Selected Works*, p.181

[40] Karl Marx, "The Eighteenth Brumaire of Louis Bonaparte", *Selected Works*, p.117

[41] Karl Marx, "The Poverty of Philosophy", in Marx and Engels, *Collected Works*, vol.6, Progress Publishers, Moscow, 1976, p.166

[42] Karl Marx, "Preface to a Contribution to the Critique of Political Economy", *Selected Works*, pp.181-82

[43] Karl Marx, "Preface to a Contribution to the Critique of Political Economy", in Marx and Engels, *Selected Works*, Progress Publishers, Moscow, 1970, p.182

[44] Frederick Engels, "Origin of Family, Private Property and the State", *Selected Works*, p.579

[45] Frederick Engels, "Origin of Family, Private Property and the State", *Selected Works*, pp. 553-556

[46] Karl Marx, "Wage Labour and Capital", *Selected Works*, p,74

[47] Frederick Engels, "Origin of Family, Private Property and the State", *Selected Works*, p. 579

[48] Karl Marx, *Capital* vol.I, Progress Publishers, Moscow, 1977, pp. 315-316 & 337-339

[49] Frederick Engels, "Origin of Family, Private Property and the State", *Selected Works*, pp. 560-563

[50] Karl Marx and Frederick Engels, "Manifesto of the Communist Party", *Selected Works*, p.37

[51] Karl Marx and Frederick Engels, "Manifesto of the Communist Party", *Selected Works*, p.37

[52] Frederick Engels, "Socialism: Utopian and Scientific", *Selected Works*, pp.383-388

[53] Karl Marx and Frederick Engels, "Manifesto of the Communist Party", *Selected Works*, p. 38.

[54] Karl Marx, *Capital*, vol.I, p.514

[55] Karl Marx, *Capital*, vol. I, Progress Publishers, Moscow, 1977, p.715

[56] Karl Marx, *Capital*, vol. I, pp. 19-20

[57] Karl Marx, "Confidential Communication", in Marx and Engels, *Selected Works*, (in three vol.) vol.2, Progress Publishers, Moscow, 1977, p.174-75

[58] Frederick Engels, "Letter to W.Borgius, January 25, 1894", Progress Publishers, Moscow, 1970, p.694

[59] Karl Marx, "The Eighteenth Brumaire of Louis Bonaparte", *Selected Works*, p.96

[60] Karl Marx, "Preface to a Contribution to the Critique Political Economy", *Selected Works*, p.182

[61] A quote given above from "Preface to a Contribution to the Critique Political Economy" is reworded.

[62] Frederick Engels, "On Social Relations in Russia", *Selected Works*, vol.2, p.406

[63] Frederick Engels, "On Social Relations in Russia", *Selected Works*, vol.2, p.409.

[64] Karl Marx, "Contribution to the Critique of Hegel's Philosophy of Law", in Marx and Engels, *Collected Works*, vol.3, Progress Publishers, Moscow, 1975, p.7

[65] Karl Marx, "Contribution to the Critique of Hegel's Philosophy of Law", *Collected Works*, vol.3, pp.5-7

[66] Karl Marx, "Contribution to the Critique of Hegel's Philosophy of Law", *Collected Works*, vol.3, p.49

[67] Karl Marx, "Contribution to the Critique of Hegel's Philosophy of Law", *Collected Works*, vol.3, p.45

[68] Karl Marx, "Contribution to the Critique of Hegel's Philosophy of Law", *Collected Works*, vol.3, p.47

[69] Frederick Engels, "The Origin of the Family, Private Property and the State", in Marx and Engels, *Selected Works,* (in one vol), Progress Publishers, Moscow, 1970, p.528

[70] Frederick Engels, "The Origin of the Family, Private Property and the State", *Selected Works*, p.528

[71] Karl Marx and Frederick Engels, "Manifesto of the Communist Party", *Selected Works*, p.53

[72] Karl Marx and Frederick Engels, "The German Ideology", in Marx and Engels, *Collected Works*, vol.5, Progress Publishers, Moscow, 1976, p.59

[73] Karl Marx and Frederick Engels, "Manifesto of the Communist Party", *Selected Works*, p.37

[74] Frederick Engels, "Apropos of Working-Class Political Action", in Marx and Engels, *Selected Works*, Progress Publishers, Moscow, 1970, p.310

[75] Karl Marx, "Critique of the Gotha Programme", *Selected Works*, p.319

[76] Frederick Engels, "Introduction to The Civil War in France", *Selected Works*, p.259

[77] Karl Marx and Frederick Engels, "Manifesto of the Communist Party", *Selected Works*, p.53

[78] Frederick Engels, "Origin of Family, Private Property and the State", *Selected Works*, p.579

[79] Frederick Engels, "Socialism: Utopian and Scientific", *Selected Works*, p.424

ABOUT THE AUTHOR

Geo Jomaria

Geo Jomaria is the pen name of George Joseph M, Associate Professor of Philosophy, Arul Anandar College, Madurai, Tamil Nadu, India. He did a comparative research on Marx and Gandhi on their approach to modernity and published it in 2001, and contributed an article on "Ideology", in ACPI Encyclopedia of Philosophy. Following are Some of the articles: "Cosmotheandric Vision: Critique of Modernity and Some Prejudices", "Beyond Secularism towards Integration", "Modern Attitudes to Cosmic Revelations: A Critique", "Re-presentation of the Enlightenment in the Postcolonial Indian Context", "Work in Panikkar's Vision", "Secularism: Strength of the Strong in the Indian Panorama", "Monopolization of Democracy" "An Aesthetic Theory towards the Hegemony of the Subaltern" etc. He did a project under University Grants Commission, Govt. of India on An Ethnomethodological Enquiry into the Principles of a Harmonious Society with Special Reference to Madurai and participated international conferences in Italy and Japan. geojomaria@gmail.com

Printed in Great Britain
by Amazon